REVISE BTEC NATIONAL
Sport and Exercise Science

REVISION WORKBOOK

Series Consultant: Harry Smith

Authors: Laura Fisher, Katie Jones, Tracy Richardson, Louise Sutton and Danielle Toward

A note from the publisher

While the publishers have made every attempt to ensure that advice on the qualification and its assessment is accurate, the official specification and associated assessment guidance materials are the only authoritative source of information and should always be referred to for definitive guidance.

This qualification is reviewed on a regular basis and may be updated in the future. Any such updates that affect the content of this Revision Workbook will be outlined at www.pearsonfe.co.uk/BTECchanges.

For the full range of Pearson revision titles across KS2, KS3, GCSE, Functional Skills, AS/A Level and BTEC visit:
www.pearsonschools.co.uk/revise

Published by Pearson Education Limited, 80 Strand, London, WC2R 0RL.

www.pearsonschoolsandfecolleges.co.uk

Copies of official specifications for all Pearson qualifications may be found on the website: qualifications.pearson.com

Text and illustrations © Pearson Education Ltd 2017
Typeset and illustrated by Kamae Design
Produced by Out of House Publishing
Cover illustration by Eoin Coveney
Picture research by Alison Prior

The rights of Laura Fisher, Katie Jones, Tracy Richardson, Louise Sutton and Danielle Toward to be identified as authors of this work has been asserted by them in accordance with the Copyright, Designs and Patents Act 1988.

Subject consultant: Katherine Howard

First published 2017

British Library Cataloguing in Publication Data
A catalogue record for this book is available from the British Library

ISBN 978 1 292 15043 7

Copyright notice
All rights reserved. No part of this publication may be reproduced in any form or by any means (including photocopying or storing it in any medium by electronic means and whether or not transiently or incidentally to some other use of this publication) without the written permission of the copyright owner, except in accordance with the provisions of the Copyright, Designs and Patents Act 1988 or under the terms of a licence issued by the Copyright Licensing Agency, Barnard's Inn, 86 Fetter Lane, London EC4A 1EN (www.cla.co.uk). Applications for the copyright owner's written permission should be addressed to the publisher.

Acknowledgements
The authors and publisher would like to thank the following individuals and organisations for permission to reproduce photographs:

Getty Images: FogStock / Vico Images / Alin Dragulin 54, Stuart Franklin / FIFA 45

All other images © Pearson Education

Notes from the publisher

1. While the publishers have made every attempt to ensure that advice on the qualification and its assessment is accurate, the official specification and associated assessment guidance materials are the only authoritative source of information and should always be referred to for definitive guidance.

Pearson examiners have not contributed to any sections in this resource relevant to examination papers for which they have responsibility.

2. Pearson has robust editorial processes, including answer and fact checks, to ensure the accuracy of the content in this publication, and every effort is made to ensure this publication is free of errors. We are, however, only human, and occasionally errors do occur. Pearson is not liable for any misunderstandings that arise as a result of errors in this publication, but it is our priority to ensure that the content is accurate. If you spot an error, please do contact us at resourcescorrections@pearson.com so we can make sure it is corrected.

Websites
Pearson Education Limited is not responsible for the content of any external internet sites. It is essential for tutors to preview each website before using it in class so as to ensure that the URL is still accurate, relevant and appropriate. We suggest that tutors bookmark useful websites and consider enabling students to access them through the school/college intranet.

Introduction

This Workbook has been designed to help you revise the skills you may need for the externally assessed units of your course. Remember that you won't necessarily be studying all the units included here – it will depend on the qualification you are taking.

BTEC Level 3 National Qualification	Externally assessed units
For both: Extended Certificate Foundation Diploma	2 Functional Anatomy 3 Applied Sport and Exercise Pyschology
Diploma	1 Sport and Exercise Physiology 2 Functional Anatomy 3 Applied Sport and Exercise Psychology
Extended Diploma	1 Sport and Exercise Physiology 2 Functional Anatomy 3 Applied Sport and Exercise Psychology 13 Nutrition for Sport and Exercise Performance

Your Workbook

Each unit in this Workbook contains either one or two sets of revision questions or revision tasks, to help you **revise the skills** you may need in your assessment. The selected content, outcomes, questions and answers used in each unit are provided to help you to revise content and ways of applying your skills. Ask your tutor or check the Pearson website for the most up-to-date **Sample Assessment Material** and **Mark Schemes** to get an indication of the structure of your actual assessment and what this requires of you. The detail of the actual assessment may change so always make sure you are up to date.

This Workbook will often include one or more useful features that explain or break down longer questions or tasks. Remember that these features won't appear in your actual assessment!

> Grey boxes like this contain **hints and tips** about ways that you might complete a task, interpret a brief, understand a concept or structure your responses.

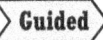 This icon will appear next to an **example partial answer** to a revision question or revision task. You should read the partial answer carefully, then complete it in your own words.

> This is a **revision activity**. It will help you understand some of the skills needed to complete the revision task or question.

> 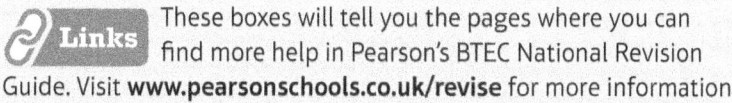 These boxes will tell you the pages where you can find more help in Pearson's BTEC National Revision Guide. Visit **www.pearsonschools.co.uk/revise** for more information.

There is often space on the pages of this Workbook for you to write in. However, if you are carrying out research and making ongoing notes, you may want to use separate paper. Similarly, some units may be assessed through submission of digital files, or on screen, rather than on paper. Ask your tutor or check the Pearson website for the most up-to-date details.

Contents

Unit 1: Sport and Exercise Physiology
- 2   Revision paper 1 (guided)
- 21   Revision paper 2

Unit 2: Functional Anatomy
- 38   Revision paper 1 (guided)
- 50   Revision paper 2

Unit 3: Applied Sport and Exercise Psychology
- 63   Revision activities (guided)
- 71   Revision questions

Unit 13: Nutrition for Sport and Exercise Performance
- 90   Revision activities (guided)
- 107   Revision questions

Answers
- 118   Unit 1
- 123   Unit 2
- 126   Unit 3
- 133   Unit 13

A small bit of small print

Pearson publishes Sample Assessment Material and the Specification on its website. This is the official content and this book should be used in conjunction with it. The questions in this book have been written to help you practise the knowledge and skills you will require for your assessment. Remember: the real assessment may not look like this.

Unit 1: Sport and Exercise Physiology

Your exam

Unit 1 will be assessed through an exam, which will be set by Pearson. You will need to use your understanding of exercise physiology in normal conditions and in different environmental conditions to answer a number of short- and long-answer questions.

Your Revision Workbook

> This Workbook is designed to **revise skills** that might be needed in your exam. The selected content, outcomes, questions and answers are provided to help you revise content and ways of applying your skills. Ask your tutor or check the Pearson website for the most up-to-date Sample Assessment Material and Mark Scheme to get an indication of the structure of your actual exam and what this requires of you. The detail of the actual exam may change so always make sure you are up to date.

To support your revision, this Workbook contains revision questions to help you revise the skills that might be needed in your exam.

Question focus

Each question will relate to a content area in the specification:
- responses of the body systems to a single sport or exercise session
- fatigue and how the body recovers from exercise
- adaptations of the body systems to exercise
- environmental factors and sport and exercise performance.

Questions may start with a scenario that relates to an individual and gives different information about the person as you progress.

Types of questions

There is guidance in this Workbook for the skills involved in answering the following types of questions.
- Give
- Identify
- State/Name
- Describe
- Explain
- Analyse
- Assess
- Discuss
- Evaluate
- To what extent

> **Links** To help you revise skills that might be needed in your Unit 1 exam, this Workbook contains two sets of revision questions starting on pages 2 and 21. The first is guided and models good techniques to help you develop your skills. The second gives you the opportunity to apply the skills you have developed. See the introduction on page iii for more information on features included to help you revise.

Unit 1
Guided

Revision paper 1

To support your revision, this Workbook contains revision tests to help you revise the skills that might be needed in your exam. Ask your tutor or check the Pearson website for the most up-to-date Sample Assessment Material to get an idea of the structure of your exam and what this requires of you. Details of the actual exam may change so always make sure you are up to date.

Answer ALL questions. Write your answers in the spaces provided.

1 a) Joe is an experienced member of his local gym club and participates in a range of fitness classes. His favourite exercise class is spinning which he does three times a week. Table 1 shows Joe's weekly training programme:

Day of the week	Time	Activity
Monday	07:30–08:15	Advanced spinning class
Tuesday	17:00–18:00	Weight training – upper body
Wednesday	07:30–08:15 18:00–19:00	Advanced spinning class Body Combat
Thursday		Rest day
Friday	17:00–18:00	Weight training – lower body
Saturday	08:30–09:15 18:00–19:00	Advanced spinning class Body Combat
Sunday	12:00–13:30	Abs/core workout and 10 km continuous running

Table 1

Explain how Joe's muscular system would respond to this training programme. **3 marks**

When responding to **explain** questions, show your **understanding** by making a point or statement and linking it with a justification that expands the point.

> **Guided**
>
> Joe's training programme will recruit muscle fibres as the muscles are put under physical stress, helping the muscles to grow and adapt in size.
>
> The process of vasoconstriction and vasodilation will increase ....
>
> ....
>
> ....
>
> When under stress, Joe's muscles will contract and relax against each other causing ....
>
> ....
>
> ....

2

Links See pages 3, 4 and 15 of the Revision Guide to revise muscular system responses to training.

1 b) Joe wears a heart rate monitor when he is training. He has noticed that his heart rate increases by an average of 9 beats per minute before he starts training.

Explain why Joe's heart rate increases just before he starts each exercise session. **3 marks**

Your answer to this **explain** question should show your understanding of why Joe's heart rate increases and go on to link it with a justification that expands the point.

Guided

An initial increase is seen in Joe's heart rate, called an anticipatory rise, because ....,

....

....

This results in an increase in blood flow which ....

....

....

This process is a sub-conscious action which is used to ....

....

Links See pages 9 and 16 of the Revision Guide to revise factors affecting heart rate.

1 c) Joe often experiences symptoms of fatigue after completing a week's training programme.

Explain **two** ways Joe's musculoskeletal system can reduce the effect of fatigue after completing his exercise programme. **4 marks**

To answer this question, state **two ways**, and **explain** and **expand** how each reduces the effect of fatigue. Ensure you choose two ways that you can properly explain.

Guided

1 Through training, Joe's ligaments and tendons have been subjected to an array of physical stresses which cause slight damage. The body produces collagen to heal the damage caused by the stress exercise places on them. This helps to strengthen the ligaments and tendons making them more resistant to fatigue.

2 ....

....

....

....

Links See page 26 of the Revision Guide to revise the effects of fatigue on the musculoskeletal system.

Unit 1
Guided

1 d) Joe's training programme uses both anaerobic and aerobic energy production.

Evaluate the effectiveness of the energy system continuum that Joe will use throughout his training regime in providing him with a constant supply of energy.

10 marks

> In **evaluate** questions, you need to **review** information before bringing it together to form a **conclusion**. You need to give your judgement and support it. You should consider **strengths and weaknesses**, **alternative actions** and **relevant data** or **information**, e.g. of a theory, process or system.

You can produce a quick **thought plan** to help tackle questions that need longer answers. You could complete the plan below to get you started. You should refer to both aerobic and anaerobic energy systems, the duration of each system, the relationships between each energy system and the by-products that are produced by each system.

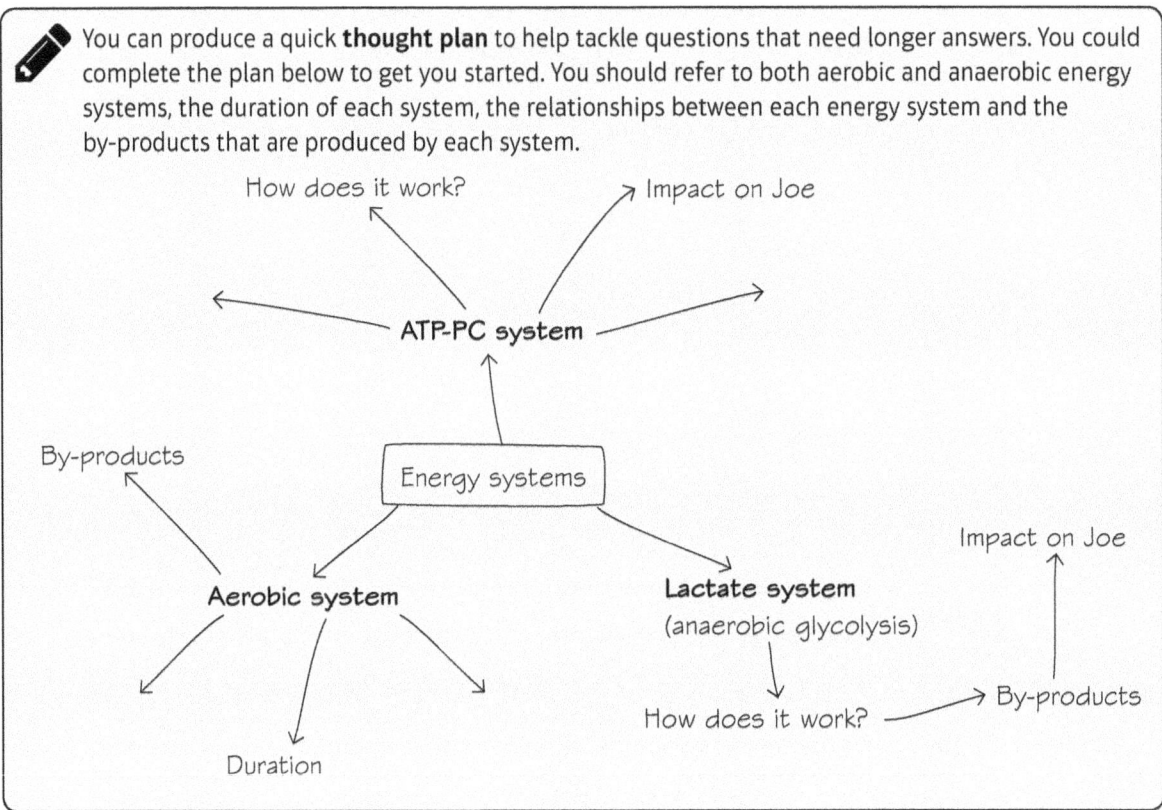

> **Guided**

Joe's fitness training programme will use all three energy systems which support the aerobic and anaerobic demands of each exercise. For Joe to be successful he needs to rely on the ATP–PC system, lactate system and aerobic energy system.

ATP–PC is the first energy system which provides enough power for a few seconds of all-out exercise. The energy system relies on ....

....

....

The ATP–PC system helps Joe with his training programme because it produces ....

....

The by-products produced by this system are ....

....

These molecules ....

....

There is a small amount of creatine phosphate in our body. This limits the ....

....

The second energy system that Joe will use is the lactate system. This is also known as anaerobic glycolysis. This energy system ....

....

....

This energy system is important because ....

....

The by-products produced by this system are ....

These by-products will affect Joe's performance because ....

....

....

....

The final energy system to be evaluated is the aerobic system. This system lasts for hours as it relies on a constant supply of oxygen.

Carbon dioxide and water are by-products for this energy system which uses

....

The aerobic energy system works by ....

....

....

....

This energy system will affect Joe's performance by ....

....

To summarise, energy systems are viewed as a continuum as ....

....

....

....

Links See pages 18–22 of the Revision Guide to revise the energy system continuum.

Total for Question 1 = 20 marks

Unit 1
Guided

2 a) Gabriella is a triathlete who is competing in the 24-hour Ironman World Championship in Hawaii. The event involves three stages.
Stage one: 2.4 mile swim in open water
Stage two: 112 mile bike ride across mountain terrain with high winds
Stage three: 26.2 mile run through the capital city

Describe what will happen to Gabriella's a-VO$_2$ diff between stage one and stage two. **3 marks**

> When responding to **describe** questions, give an account, or details, of 'something' or give an account of a 'process'.
> In this question, think about the difference in the amount of oxygen found between arterial and venous blood. Describe why the oxygen levels would have differences in intensities between stage 1 and stage 2.

Guided

Arteriovenous oxygen difference (a-VO$_2$ diff) is the difference in the amount of oxygen found

....

The difference between stage 1 and stage 2 will ....

....

....

....

The difference between arterial and venous blood increases due to the ....

....

....

> **Links** To revise arteriovenous oxygen difference (a-VO$_2$ diff), see page 13 of the Revision Guide.

Unit 1
Guided

2 b) As Gabriella's Ironman event will take place over a 24-hour period, it is essential that she has a sufficient supply of nutrients in her body to support sustained energy production.

Explain what nutritional substances can be consumed by Gabriella during the Ironman event which will support her in completing the challenge.

4 marks

You need to show your **understanding** of what constitutes a nutritional substance, i.e. what makes up a balanced diet. Think about the **demands of the event** and the **methods** by which Gabriella can take on board nutrients, for example shakes and gels. Consider what the **nutritional substances do**, for example carbohydrates and proteins. **Explain** how these will support Gabriella to complete the Ironman challenge.

Due to the duration of Gabriella's event taking place over a 24-hour period, there will be limited

opportunities to ....

Therefore, Gabriella will need ....

Protein is needed to ....

....

Gabriella will also need a supply of ....

....

Links See page 25 of the Revision Guide to revise information on nutritional substances and their role in supporting aerobic performance.

Unit 1 — Guided

2 c) Part way through stage 3 of the Ironman event, Gabriella begins to experience a significant reduction in her race pace. Her muscles are aching and she is struggling to make repeated muscle contractions.

Explain the effects that neuromuscular fatigue would have on Gabriella's race performance.

3 marks

You need to **explain** what neuromuscular fatigue is, what units are involved and how a reduction in these units **impacts** on Gabriella's performance.

> **Guided**

Neuromuscular fatigue is common after exposure to ....

The motor units from the central nervous system ....

....

The loss of ....

....

Acetylcholine is released by the ....

....

However, when this gets depleted the muscle fibres are unable to ....

....

Links See page 23 of the Revision Guide to revise what neuromuscular fatigue is and the effect it has on performance.

2 d) The race organisers have issued a formal warning informing athletes that temperatures are expected to peak at 39°C, accompanied by humid conditions.

Analyse the effect that exposure to excessive heat will have on Gabriella's body and performance.

10 marks

When responding to **analyse** questions, carry out a detailed examination in order to discover the **meaning** or **essential features** of a theme, topic or situation. You will need to **break something down** into its component parts and examine **factors** methodically and in detail. In addition, you will have to identify separate factors, say how they are related and explain how each one contributes to the topic.

You can produce a quick **thought plan** to help tackle questions that need longer answers. You could complete the plan below to get you started.

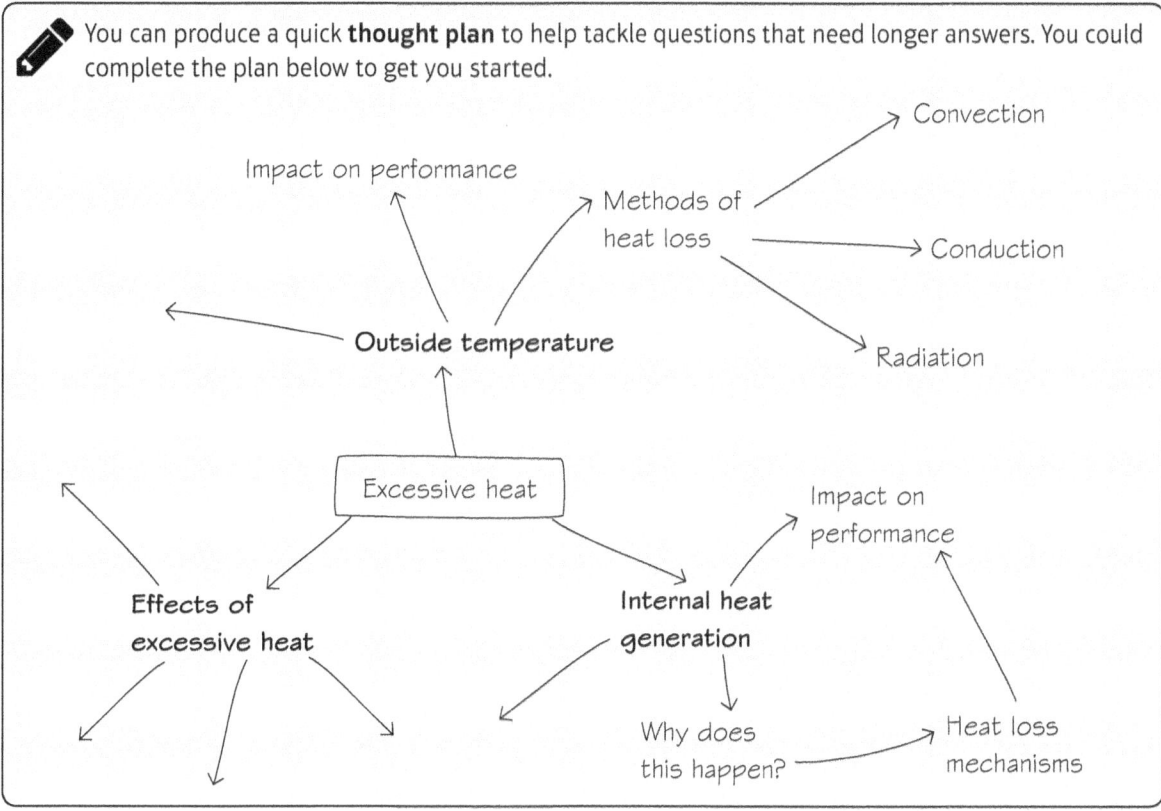

Guided

The predicted outside temperature for Gabriella's competition is high. As Gabriella exercises, she will also be generating heat as a waste product of exercise. To help combat the excess heat, Gabriella's body will work hard to cool ....

....

Heat will be lost through ....

....

....

....

....

....

Unit 1
Guided

When Gabriella sweats she will lose electrolytes and water during the cooling process. The more Gabriella sweats the greater the depletion of electrolytes. It is important that ....

....

....

....

....

....

....

The temperature that is predicted for Gabriella's race is considered to be an extreme temperature. Exposure to extreme heat temperatures will produce ....

....

....

....

....

Based on the predicted temperatures, it is clear that Gabriella will suffer from ....

....

....

....

....

Dehydration can cause ....

....

Links See pages 45–50 of the Revision Guide to revise what excessive heat is, how the body adapts to it and the impact of excessive heat on performance.

Total for Question 2 = 20 marks

3 a) Parvez is a busy full-time student who is juggling college work and a part-time job. Parvez carries out high-intensity interval training (HIIT) to help him improve his cardiovascular fitness. He has developed an eight-week training programme which targets all the major muscle groups including his core.

For Parvez's first five-week period, he completed three training sessions a week working on all major muscle groups.

For the final three weeks, Parvez completed HIIT training every other day allowing the second day to become a rest day.

Parvez completed a range of tests prior to completing this training programme so that he could see how much he improves. Table 2 shows the range of tests used and the results at key stages.

	Week 1	Week 4	Week 8
Weight	99.3 kg	89.5 kg	91.6 kg
Body fat	31.2%	28.4%	24.2%
VO$_2$ max	33 ml/kg/min	36 ml/kg/min	39 ml/kg/min
1RM bench press	45 kg	50 kg	54 kg
1 RM back squat	75 kg	87 kg	91 kg

Table 2

Give **three** examples of the different muscle fibres recruited by Parvez to perform his HIIT training exercises.

3 marks

When answering **give** questions, provide **examples**, **justifications**, and/or **reasons** for something.

Think about the **three types of muscle fibres** and **apply** these to the examples that Parvez uses in his HIIT training.

1 Type I muscle fibres will be used when Parvez is working at a low intensity for a long duration, e.g. jogging.

2 Type IIa muscle fibres will be used to provide ....

....

....

3 Type IIx muscle fibres will be used to provide ....

....

....

Links See pages 3–4 of the Revision Guide to revise muscle fibre recruitment and exercise effects.

Unit 1 Guided

3 b) During HIIT exercises, the nervous system plays a crucial role in ensuring that the body continues to respond to motor neurons sent from the central nervous system. The respiratory system responds by ensuring that Parvez has enough oxygen in his blood to supply the working muscles, assisting them to make repeated explosive contractions without fatigue.

Explain why the onset of blood lactate (OBLA) occurs during Parvez's HIIT training sessions.

4 marks

You could **break** the answer into **two parts**. First, explain what OBLA is and when it occurs. Then for the second part you need to relate your answer to Parvez's training sessions. Think about the intensity of the exercise and the energy system that HIIT training predominantly uses.

The onset of blood lactate (OBLA) occurs when the level of lactate in the blood reaches 4 mmol/L

and above. 4 mmol/L is known as the ....

OBLA happens when ....

....

....

....

When exercise continues when blood lactate is above 4 mmol/L ....

....

....

With HIIT training, Parvez will experience OBLA ....

....

....

The rest period between the work periods ....

....

Links See pages 20 and 22 of the Revision Guide to revise the onset of blood lactate.

Unit 1
Guided

3 c) After eight weeks of HIIT training, Parvez reviewed the effectiveness of his training programme. He found that, after reducing his number of rest days, the gains in training decreased as compared to his improvement between weeks 1 and 4.

Parvez also found it a struggle getting up and down the stairs when he increased his training.

He decided to complete a further four-week training programme but reduce the training frequency to three times a week, using the same measures as before. The results are shown in Table 3.

	Week 8	Week 12
Weight	91.6 kg	83.3 kg
Body fat	24.2%	21.8%
VO_2 max	39 ml/kg/min	56 ml/kg/min
1RM bench press	54 kg	75 kg
1 RM back squat	91 kg	109 kg

Table 3

Fatigue has had an impact on Parvez's ability to be able to significantly improve his cardiovascular fitness in week 8.

Explain, using Table 3, how fatigue has affected Parvez's week 8 results. **3 marks**

You need to use the **results in Table 3** and **compare the differences** between **week 8 and week 12**. You can also look at the results from **Table 2** (page 11) for **week 4** as a comparison. For this type of question, you need to be able to explain the **effectiveness** of a change and whether it has had a **positive**, **negative** or **neutral impact**. It is essential that you use information from the **table** to construct your answer.

> **Guided**

Energy sources can become depleted in the training sessions and within the recovery period.

....

....

Parvez will experience delayed onset of muscle soreness (DOMS). This is a discomfort ....

....

....

The pain and stiffness experienced as a result of DOMS ....

....

....

....

> **Links** See pages 23–26 of the Revision Guide to revise the effect of fatigue on exercise performance.

Unit 1
Guided

3 d) To what extent has the revised training programme affected Parvez's cardiovascular and muscular systems? `10 marks`

> When answering **to what extent** questions, **review information then bring it together** and form a **conclusion** or a **judgement**. It is important that your answer includes a **balanced** and **reasoned** argument.

You can produce a quick **thought plan** to help tackle questions that need longer answers. You could complete the plan below to get you started.

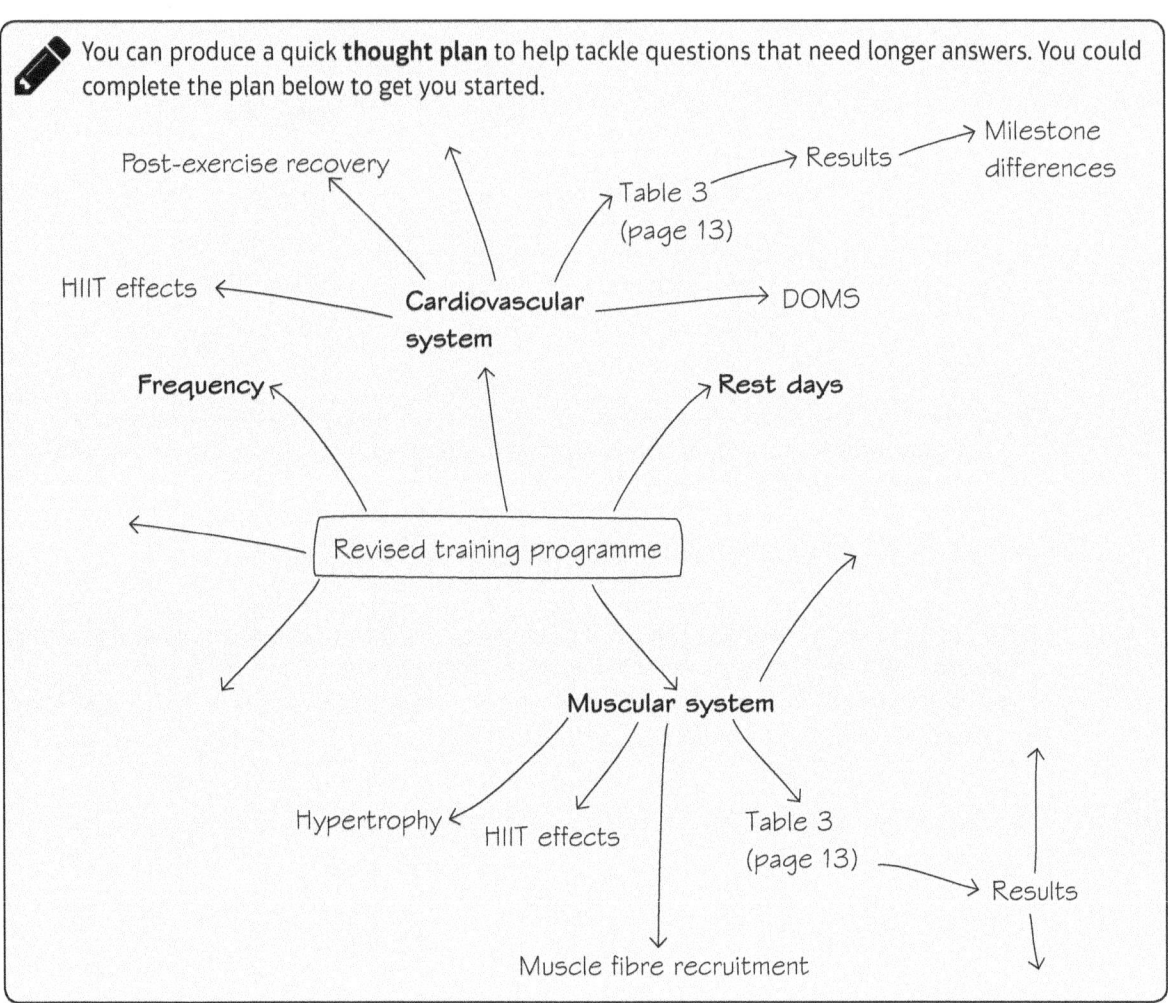

Guided

Over the 12-week training period, Parvez has improved his VO_2 max result at each stage.

However, between weeks 4 and 8 the change in test results was small.

An increase in Parvez's VO_2 max shows ....

....

....

The higher the VO_2 max, ...

A greater VO_2 max allows Parvez to continue ....

....

An increase in Parvez's VO_2 max also assists him to ....

....

Parvez will be able to withstand a higher amount of ....

....

The change in frequency of the training programme, back to three times a week, has enabled Parvez to be able to continue to make progress in improving his cardiovascular fitness. The change in frequency has also ....

....

....

EPOC becomes more effective at minimising the effect of ....

....

Parvez's results in week 12 have improved since the training sessions were reduced to three per week as opposed to every other day between weeks 5 and 8. By reducing the frequency ....

....

....

Providing Parvez has a sufficient amount of rest in between training sessions ....

....

....

As a result of hypertrophy, Parvez's muscles will be able to generate ....

....

....

Over time, Parvez's muscles will adapt to HIIT. HIIT uses heavy loads, i.e. body weight exercises. This causes Type IIa muscle fibres to ....

....

....

....

Links See pages 3, 4 and 9–15 of the Revision Guide to revise the effects of exercise on the body systems and pages 30–37 to revise how adaptations impact exercise performance.

Total for Question 3 = 20 marks

Unit 1
Guided

4 a) Naseem is a county level swimmer. Her favourite race to compete in is 200 m butterfly. She is currently training for national trials and is working hard to reduce her 200 m time. She trains for 2 hours a day, five days a week. Her training sessions consist of both land and pool training. These training sessions consist mainly of aerobic activities.

Identify **three** ways in which Naseem's cardiovascular system responds to aerobic training. **3 marks**

> When answering **identify** questions, you may need to assess **factual information** that may require a single word answer, although sometimes a few words or a maximum of a single sentence are required. Be careful not to spend too much time on a long and detailed answer as this is **not** needed.

1 Vasoconstriction – occurs in blood vessels that do not need an enhanced blood supply during exercise, while vasodilation occurs in active muscles by ....

....

....

2 Increased cardiac output – occurs as the volume of blood pumped out per minute ....

....

....

....

....

3 ....

....

> **Links** See pages 9–13 of the Revision Guide to revise cardiovascular responses to exercise.

Unit 1
Guided

4 b) Explain **two** ways Naseem's aerobic energy system adapts to both land and pool training sessions. **4 marks**

> This question is specific to **aerobic energy systems** so it is important that your answer **focuses** on this and not any other energy system. You need to select two adaptations that occur during exercise training sessions. Think about the demands of the sport – what will help Naseem's performance to improve?

> **Guided**

1 During the first few minutes of Naseem's training session, in the pool or on land, her body will be fuelled by anaerobic metabolism due to ....

....

....

....

2 Naseem's training programme, in the pool or on land, will be fuelled by carbohydrate and fat stores which ....

....

....

....

....

> **Links** See pages 21 and 37 of the Revision Guide to revise the aerobic energy system and adaptations.

Unit 1 Guided

4 c) Naseem has 48 hours until she competes in her national trial. It is important that she is both physically and mentally prepared for the event. As part of her training cycle, she is also given nutritional guidelines as to what food groups she should eat and when, in order to optimise her performance.

Explain why it is important that Naseem consumes a high carbohydrate diet over the next 48 hours. **3 marks**

When answering this question, **explain three points** to say **why it is important** that Naseem consumes a **high carbohydrate** diet on the lead up to competition.

Naseem will use her glycogen stores in the muscles to break down the glycogen enzymes into glucose which ....

....

....

An increased level of carbohydrates in Naseem's muscles will provide Naseem with ....

....

....

By having more carbohydrates in the body, she will be able to ....

....

Links See page 21 of the Revision Guide to revise aerobic metabolism.

Unit 1
Guided

4 d) Following completion of her three-month training cycle, Naseem performs a series of tests to measure the effectiveness of it. Naseem and her coach use this information from the tests to review how effective the training programme has been. Table 4 shows the results of her cardiovascular and respiratory functioning at the start and at the end of her training cycle.

Measure	Start of training cycle	End of training cycle
Forced vital capacity	4.0 L	4.7 L
VO_2 max	46 ml/kg/min	51 ml/kg/min
Body fat	22.1%	16.9%
Resting heart rate	56	54

Table 4

Discuss the effect that Naseem's training programme has had on her cardiovascular and respiratory systems and how this will affect Naseem's fitness for her national swimming trials. **10 marks**

When answering **discuss** questions, **identify** the issue, situation, problem or argument that is being assessed in the question given. You need to **explore** all aspects and **investigate** it fully. Come to a **conclusion** that sums up the **outcome** of the discussion, at the end.

You can produce a quick **thought plan** to help tackle questions that need longer answers. You could complete the plan below to get you started.

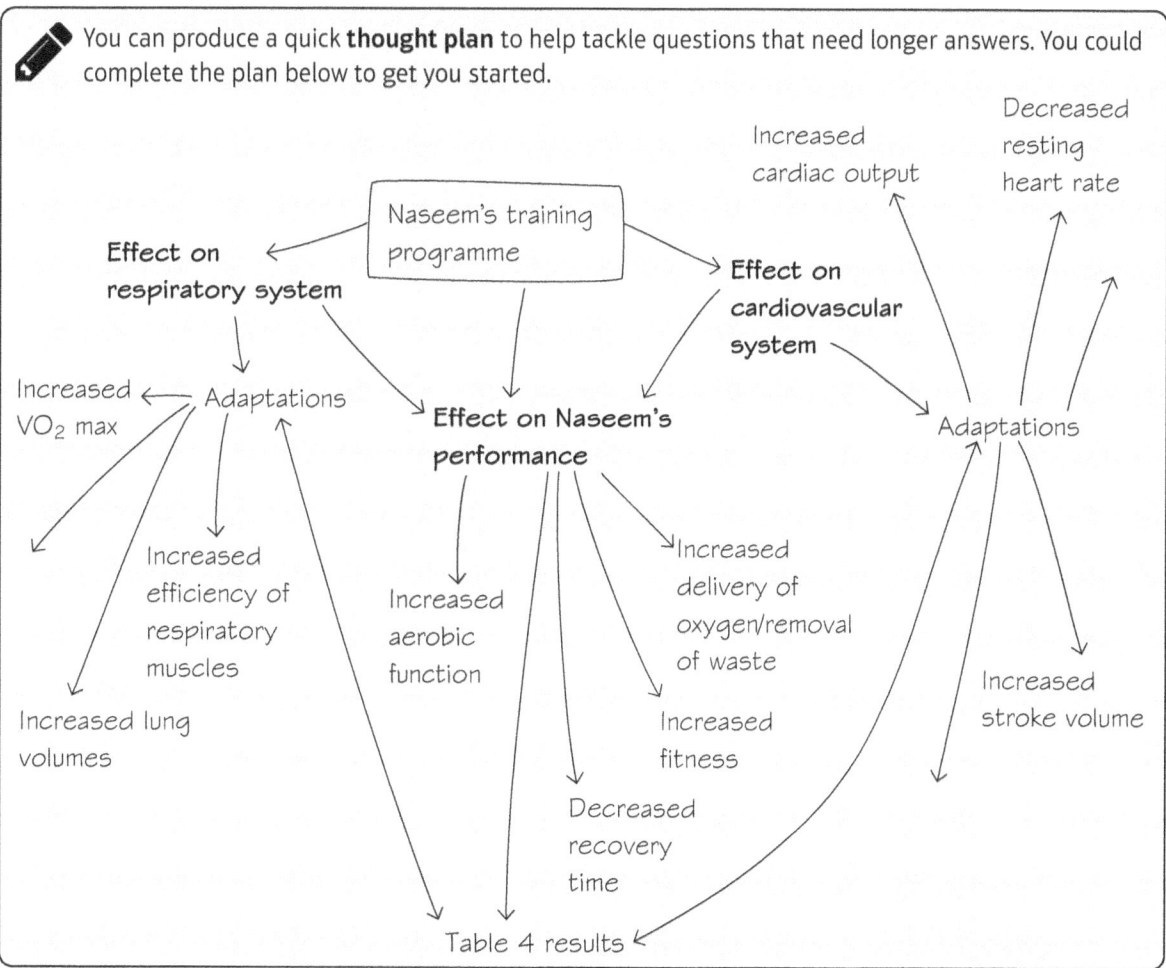

Guided

Naseem's training programme has been effective at putting the cardiovascular and respiratory

systems under increased pressure causing them to ....

....

This is supported by the results in Table 4 in which all results have shown ....

....

Through sustained aerobic training Naseem will have increased her stroke volume which slows down her ....

This adaptation can be evidenced in the decrease in Naseem's ....

Naseem's maximal cardiac output will assist in supplying the working muscles with ....
....
....

Table 4 shows that there has been a significant improvement in her lung function volumes. This will assist Naseem to breathe in more ....
....

The cardiovascular system becomes more efficient as the respiratory muscles increase in ....
....

The higher the contraction rate the greater the volume of air. This effect is evidenced by the 700 ml increase in the ....

Naseem's tidal volume, vital capacity and residual volume increase with sustained aerobic training. Naseem will be able to utilise the increased amount of oxygen present in the system and ....
....

The delay in the onset of blood lactate is a result of Naseem's increased VO_2 max because Naseem is able to utilise ....
....

Naseem's body will adapt and her respiratory rate will increase to aid the ....
....
....
....

Links See pages 30–37 of the Revision Guide to revise the effects of aerobic training on the cardiovascular and muscular system and the impact of the adaptations on sporting performance.

Total for Question 4 = 20 marks

END OF PAPER

TOTAL FOR PAPER 1 = 80 MARKS

Revision paper 2

Unit 1

To support your revision, this Workbook contains revision tests to help you revise the skills that might be needed in your exam. Ask your tutor or check the Pearson website for the most up-to-date Sample Assessment Material to get an idea of the structure of your exam and what this requires of you. Details of the actual exam may change so always make sure you are up to date.

Answer ALL questions. Write your answers in the spaces provided.

1 a) Leah is a CrossFit athlete. When she trains and competes, she has to complete a series of exercises, performing the most repetitions within the quickest possible time. It is high intensity, vigorous exercise incorporating muscular strength and endurance. A lot of stress is placed on her joints, so prior to training sessions and competing she always warms up.

Explain how performing a thorough warm-up prior to participating in CrossFit will help Leah to protect her joints and perform well.

3 marks

> When you are **explaining**, show your **understanding**. Make a **point** and **justify** it with a reason.

....
....
....
....
....

Links To revise synovial fluid, see page 2 of the Revision Guide.

1 b) Leah has completed an open workout to help to qualify for the regional stage of competition. She had to complete the following exercises in the quickest possible time: 55 deadlifts, 55 wall ball throws, a 55 calorie row and 55 handstand push ups, which she completed in 9 minutes and 37 seconds.

Explain how the high intensity of CrossFit affects Leah's motor unit and muscle fibre recruitment.

3 marks

....
....
....
....
....

Links To revise muscle fibre recruitment, see page 3 of the Revision Guide and see page 14 to revise motor unit recruitment.

Unit 1

1 c) CrossFit involves a variety of exercises. In Leah's next open workout, she had to complete as many sets of the following exercises as she could within 10 minutes: 25 walking lunges, 8 burpees and 8 pull-ups. As she needs to complete the most repetitions she can within the time frame, she is moving quickly at high intensity and may be prone to overstretching and become injured.

Explain **two** ways proprioceptive responses allow Leah to avoid overstretching and injury.

4 marks

1 ....
....
....
....

2 ....
....
....
....

🔗 **Links** See page 15 of the Revision Guide to revise muscle spindles and golgi tendon organs.

Unit 1

1 d) Leah has qualified for the regional competition, which involves seven different exercise challenges over three days. On day 1, one of the two challenges involves a 1000 m bike ride, 100 m handstand walk, 500 m row, 50 burpees and 10 overhead squats, which will involve muscular strength and endurance, and cardiovascular endurance.

Evaluate the effect of Leah's endocrine system upon her energy, cardiovascular, respiratory and muscular systems, and how this will affect her CrossFit competition performance.

10 marks

> When you **evaluate**, you should **review** information before bringing it together to form a **conclusion**. You need to give your **judgement** and **support** it. Your evaluation should draw on **evidence** in relation to strengths and areas to improve, and provide judgements about their **effects**.

Links To revise the endocrine system, see pages 16 and 17 of the Revision Guide.

Total for Question 1 = 20 marks

Unit 1

2 a) Jamie is a 400 m hurdler who is competing for a place in the British team. His event is intense and, due to the large number of entrants, the competition has heats, second rounds, quarter-finals, semi-finals and a final, over three days.

Describe how participating in five races over three days may cause fatigue and affect Jamie's performance.

3 marks

> When you **describe**, you should give an **account** or **details**.

....

....

....

....

....

....

Links To revise the causes of fatigue, see page 23 of the Revision Guide.

2 b) Following the completion of two days of competition, Jamie has gained a place in the final the next day. To be fully prepared and successful, he needs to get as much rest as possible if he wants to gain a place on the British team.

Explain how Jamie's body systems will recover in preparation for the next day's competition.

4 marks

....

....

....

....

....

....

....

....

....

Links To revise energy recovery, see page 24 of the Revision Guide.

25

2 c) On the day of the final, the environmental temperature increased from 29°C to 34°C, so it was essential Jamie drank enough water throughout the day.

Jamie won his race, but after competing he was fatigued, felt hot and sweated a lot. Jamie usually weighs 70 kg, but after the race he weighed 68.6 kg.

Explain how Jamie can refuel and rehydrate following his competition.

3 marks

....

....

....

....

....

....

> **Links** To revise nutrition for recovery, see page 25 of the Revision Guide and see page 26 to revise musculoskeletal recovery.

2 d) After securing a place on the team, Jamie's new training programme has progressed over a 12-week period, as shown in Table 1. Over the first six weeks, his performance improved. He maintained his performance from weeks 6–12. However, after week 12 he found that his performance level started to drop and he felt fatigued and struggled to complete his training sessions.

	Week 1	Week 6	Week 12
Training load	RPE 7/10	RPE 7–8/10	RPE 8/10
Training volume	6 days per week 1 training session per day	4 days per week 2 training sessions per day	6 days per week 2 training sessions per day
Recovery	1 day	2 days	1 day

Table 1

Analyse why Jamie's performance levels have dropped in response to increasing his training volume and training load and decreasing his recovery time.

10 marks

When you **analyse**, you need to examine the information in **detail**. Highlight **essential features** and details, and say how they are related, explaining the reasons for their effect.

Total for Question 2 = 20 marks

Unit 1

3 a) Devon is a rower. Her main event is the Olympic 2000 metre distance with a personal best time of 7 minutes and 49 seconds.

The event is very demanding, and she is training hard to better this time. Within her training programme, her training sessions include muscular strength and endurance, and anaerobic and aerobic endurance training.

During her training, the respiratory system will become more efficient, improving the delivery of oxygen and removal of carbon dioxide.

State **three** other adaptations of the respiratory system when carrying out aerobic training. **3 marks**

> When you **state** or **name**, you should give a **definition** or **relevant example**.

1 ....
....

2 ....
....

3 ....
....

🔗 **Links** To revise respiratory adaptations, see page 32 of the Revision Guide.

3 b) Devon completes regular aerobic training in excess of the duration it takes her to complete the actual event. This is to help her cardiovascular system adapt to the increased demands placed upon it during her event.

Explain the adaptations to Devon's cardiovascular system in response to the aerobic training Devon performs. **4 marks**

....
....
....
....
....
....
....
....

🔗 **Links** To revise cardiovascular adaptations, see page 33 of the Revision Guide.

3 c) Devon uses the one repetition maximum (1RM) to programme her resistance training loads and help her to monitor her progress. She works on muscular strength to help develop power and muscular endurance to help with the anaerobic nature of the event.

Training load	Training volume	Inter-set rest
80% 1RM	3 sets of 10 repetitions	3 minutes
60% 1RM	2 sets of 25 repetitions	1 minute

Table 2

Explain the endocrine system responses to training that Devon will experience from undertaking training sessions for strength and muscular endurance using the training variables in **Table 2**. **3 marks**

> When **referring to a table**, ensure that you read the **column headings** and relate this to the **information in the columns** and the **wording of the question**.

....

....

....

....

....

....

Links To revise endocrine adaptations, see page 35 of the Revision Guide.

Unit 1

3 d) In addition to 1RM, over the past 12 weeks Devon has used testing of anaerobic threshold and anaerobic power to help gauge progression within her training and determine her fitness for competitions.

Assess the influence of VO_2 max, anaerobic threshold and anaerobic power, with reference to their measurement, on Devon's performance.

10 marks

When you **assess** information, you present a **careful consideration** of factors or events that apply to a specific situation. Or you can **identify** those which are the most important or relevant, to arrive at an overall **conclusion**.

....
....
....
....
....
....
....
....
....
....
....
....
....
....
....
....
....
....
....
....
....
....
....
....
....
....
....
....

Unit 1

Links To revise measurement and effects of anaerobic threshold and anaerobic power, see page 38 of the Revision Guide.

Total for Question 3 = 20 marks

Unit 1

4 a) Asanti is a footballer and is currently away with the team for a summer warm weather training camp for six weeks prior to the start of the next season. The camp allows the players to train in warmer weather conditions, which allows them to develop and progress their training, reduce the risk of injury and provide longer daylight hours for training.

As the training camp is set above sea level, there are a number of training adaptations that Asanti will undergo during his training sessions.

State **three** initial responses of the body systems to high altitude. **3 marks**

When you **state** information, you give a **definition** or a **relevant example**.

1 ....

....

2 ....

....

3 ....

....

Links To revise body responses to high altitude, see pages 40–43 of the Revision Guide.

4 b) When Asanti is training in the mornings for about 3 hours, the environmental temperature is around 20°C, so he does become very hot.

Explain how thermoregulation affects Asanti when he is training in order to maintain homeostasis. **4 marks**

....

....

....

....

....

....

....

....

....

....

Links To revise thermoregulation, see page 45 of the Revision Guide and see page 46 to revise homeostasis.

4 c) As the six weeks progress, Asanti and his coaches have noted some changes in his performance. He is feeling less fatigued from training, and his resting breathing rate and heart rate have both decreased, resulting in a marked improvement in performance.

Explain the adaptations to altitude that Asanti's body may undergo following six weeks of training.

3 marks

....

....

....

....

....

....

Links To revise adaptations to altitude, see pages 40–43 of the Revision Guide.

4 d) As temperatures during the day can reach over 35°C, Asanti also aims to train in the early evenings as it is slightly cooler. This isn't always possible, however, particularly if a friendly fixture has been arranged. The excessive heat is very different from the environmental conditions at home, so this may have an impact on his performance over the six weeks.

Evaluate Asanti's body's adaptations to the excessive heat following the six weeks of training and the effects upon his performance.

10 marks

When you **evaluate**, you should **review** information before bringing it together to form a **conclusion**. You need to give your **judgement** and **support** it. Your evaluation should draw on **evidence** in relation to strengths and areas to improve, and provide judgements about their **effects**.

Links To revise the body's adaptations to excessive heat, see pages 48–50 of the Revision Guide and see page 47 to revise the impact of heat on performance.

Total for Question 4 = 20 marks

END OF PAPER — TOTAL FOR PAPER 2 = 80 MARKS

Unit 2: Functional Anatomy

Your exam

Unit 2 will be assessed through an exam, which will be set by Pearson. You will need to use your understanding of the anatomy of the cardiovascular, respiratory, skeletal and muscular systems. You will use your knowledge and understanding of the different systems to analyse how they produce movements in sport and exercise, including how they relate to carry out those movements. You will be asked a number of short- and long-answer questions.

Your Revision Workbook

> This Workbook is designed to **revise skills** that might be needed in your exam. The selected content, outcomes, questions and answers are provided to help you revise content and ways of applying your skills. Ask your tutor or check the Pearson website for the most up-to-date Sample Assessment Material and Mark Scheme to get an indication of the structure of your actual exam and what this requires of you. The detail of the actual exam may change so always make sure you are up to date.

To support your revision, this Workbook contains revision questions to help you revise the skills that might be needed in your exam.

Types of questions

There is guidance in this Workbook for the skills involved in answering the following types of questions.
- Give
- Identify
- Name
- State
- Describe
- Explain
- Analyse
- Assess
- Evaluate
- Discuss
- To what extent

> **Links** To help you revise skills that might be needed in your Unit 2 exam, this Workbook contains two sets of revision questions starting on pages 38 and 50. The first is guided and models good techniques to help you develop your skills. The second gives you the opportunity to apply the skills you have developed. See the introduction on page iii for more information on features included to help you revise.

Revision paper 1

> To support your revision, this Workbook contains revision tests to help you revise the skills that might be needed in your exam. Ask your tutor or check the Pearson website for the most up-to-date Sample Assessment Material to get an idea of the structure of your exam and what this requires of you. Details of the actual exam may change so always make sure you are up to date.

Answer ALL questions. Write your answers in the spaces provided.

1 State the location and function of the bundle of His. **2 marks**

> In response to **state** or **name** questions, you must give a definition or example.

Guided

The bundle of His is located in the heart and its function is ....

....

....

Links See page 71 of the Revision Guide to revise the location of the bundle of His and its role in the cardiac cycle.

Total for Question 1 = 2 marks

2 Give the meaning of the following anatomical terms.

> For this **give** question, you need to provide **definitions**. Some give questions need examples or reasons.

Guided

a) Lateral **1 mark**

Away from the mid-line of the body

b) Peripheral **1 mark**

....

....

Links See page 66 of the Revision Guide to revise definitions of anatomical language.

Total for Question 2 = 2 marks

3 Describe the function of alveoli. [2 marks]

> In response to **describe** questions, you give an **account**, or **details**, of 'something' or of a 'process'.
> Complete the description of the alveoli below, in relation to oxygen and carbon dioxide.

Guided

The alveoli are small air sacs found in the lungs and allow the transfer of ....

....

....

> **Links** See pages 72 and 74 of the Revision Guide to revise gaseous exchange and the actions of the alveoli.

Total for Question 3 = 2 marks

4 Explain **one** of the functions of the cardiovascular system when exercising. [4 marks]

> In response to **explain** questions, you should show your **understanding** by making a point or statement and linking it with a **justification** or **expansion**.
> Complete the explanation below in relation to **one** of the following: removal of waste products **or** control of blood flow.

Guided

The cardiovascular system is responsible for delivering oxygen and nutrients around the body

especially during exercise when there is higher demand. ....

....

....

....

> **Links** See page 70 of the Revision Guide for the functions of the cardiovascular system.

Total for Question 4 = 4 marks

Unit 2 Guided

5 Describe the process of the cardiac cycle. `3 marks`

> In response to this **describe** question, you should give details of the **process** and link it to exercise. Continue the answer below to describe the cardiac cycle with reference to the systolic and diastolic process.

Guided

The cardiac cycle is the blood flow through the heart to create a heartbeat. ....

....

....

....

....

....

....

> **Links** See page 71 of the Revision Guide for the process of the cardiac cycle.

Total for Question 5 = 3 marks

6 Describe the process of neuromuscular control of muscle contraction. `5 marks`

> Continue **describing** the process below with reference to the neuromuscular junction (synapse) and neurotransmitters (acetylcholine).

Guided

When an athlete wants to exercise, a message is received from the brain which then transmits to the muscles the athlete wants to use. To do this, there are nerve impulses which are an electrical current that run from the CNS (central nervous system) to the muscles. The neuromuscular junction is the place where ....

....

....

....

....

....

> **Links** See page 89 of the Revision Guide to revise neuromuscular control.

Total for Question 6 = 5 marks

7 Table 1 shows the differences between the amount of carbon dioxide inhaled and exhaled during exercise.

	Inhaled %	Exhaled at rest %	Exhaled during exercise %
Carbon dioxide	0.05	4	6

Table 1

Explain why there are differences in the carbon dioxide percentages at rest and during exercise.

4 marks

Complete the **explanation** below to demonstrate your **understanding**. The answer needs to **make a point** and then you need to **link** the statement to an **example or justification**.

Carbon dioxide is a waste product created in the process of respiration and needs to be removed from the body. During exercise the body produces more carbon dioxide and it needs to be exhaled to prevent ....

During exercise the body/muscles need more energy, so more oxygen is used which produces more ....

....

....

Links See pages 73 and 74 of the Revision Guide to revise the respiratory system.

Total for Question 7 = 4 marks

Unit 2 Guided

8 Tanya takes part in CrossFit competitions. She is trying to maximise her training for the regional event and needs to know more about different types of training.

Explain the difference between isometric and isotonic (concentric and eccentric) muscle contractions.

4 marks

Responses to **explain** questions may require you to show your understanding of differences between processes in the context of an individual's sport and training needs.

Continue the response below to explain concentric contractions, eccentric contracts and isometric contractions.

Muscles contract depending on the particular needs of the exercise. Most exercises in CrossFit require isotonic contractions as the length of the muscle changes throughout the exercise.

Concentric contractions involve ....

....

Eccentric contractions are where ....

....

Isometric contractions involve the muscle ....

....

 **Links** See page 91 of the Revision Guide to revise information on types of muscle contraction.

Total for Question 8 = 4 marks

9 Describe movement of muscles in antagonistic muscle pairs. **4 marks**

> In response to this question, you must **include details** of the following **four** key points: muscles work in pairs; the role of the agonist; the role of the antagonist; the roles of synergists and fixators.

....
....
....
....
....
....
....
....
....

> **Links** See page 96 of the Revision Guide to revise antagonistic muscle pairs and their use in sport and exercise.

Total for Question 9 = 4 marks

10 Figure 1 shows an athlete performing a high jump.

Figure 1

Analyse the role of the musculoskeletal system at the knee and the vertebral column during the take-off phase of the high jump.

8 marks

> You could start by identifying the key components of each movement, and relating them to achieving the take-off movement in Figure 1.
>
> You can produce a quick **thought plan** for your analysis, using the plan below to get you started.

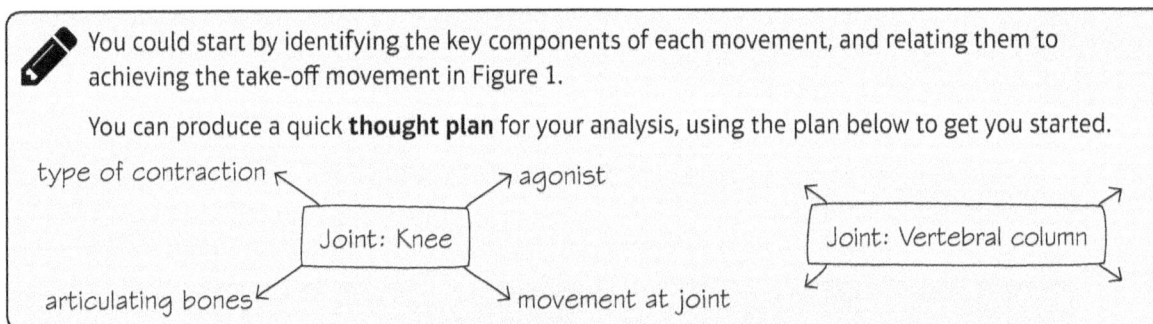

Guided

The bones and joints in the skeleton, as well as the muscles, will need to work together to produce the required movement for the high jump as highlighted in Figure 1.

The knee

In the knee, during take-off, the articulating bones are the ....

The movement at the hinge joint is ....

The agonist muscle working to produce this movement is the ....

The type of contraction in the agonist is ....

The vertebral column

In the take-off phase, the .... will be the bones involved in

producing the movement.

The movements at the cartilaginous joints in the vertebrae are ....

The agonists creating this movement are the ....

The type of contraction in the agonists is ....

The muscles and bones must work together so the athlete ....

....

> **Links** To revise types of bone, see page 82 of the Revision Guide and see pages 84–86 for joints involved in movement, page 91 for types of muscle contraction and page 96 for antagonistic muscle pairs.

Total for Question 10 = 8 marks

Unit 2
Guided

11 Figure 2 shows Fara taking a penalty for England.

Figure 2

Analyse how the axial and appendicular skeleton allows the ranges of movement necessary at the trunk, knee and ankle of Fara's striking leg.

12 marks

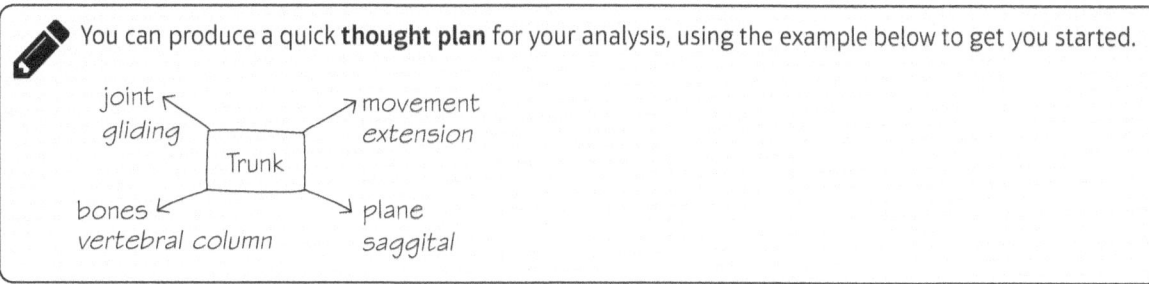

> **Guided**

Fara's striking leg is in the .... phase of the movement.

Trunk

The type of joint is .... and the movement at the joint is ....

The bones are the .... and the plane of movement is ....

Ankle

The type of joint is .... and the movement at the joint is............................

The bones are the .... and the plane of movement is............................

Knee

The type of joint is .... and the movement at the joint is ....

The bones are the .... and the plane of movement is ....

The three joints all need to work effectively to ensure Fara can ....

....

Links To revise the location of bones, see page 79 of the Revision Guide and see pages 85 and 99 for types of joint and movement and pages 97–98 for planes of movement.

Total for Question 11 = 12 marks

Unit 2
Guided

12 Figure 3 shows an athlete performing a squat.

Figure 3

Analyse the movements required at the knee, hip and ankle to perform positions A to B during a squat.

20 marks

> You can produce a quick plan for your analysis, using the table below to get you started.
>
> | Joint | Bones | Movement | Agonist | Plane | Type of contraction |
> |-------|-------|----------|---------|-------|---------------------|
> | | | | | | |
> | | | | | | |
> | | | | | | |

Guided

To produce the movement at position B in the picture, the hip, knee and ankle must move at the same time to ensure the technique is correct.

Knee

The type of joint at the knee is a hinge joint which allows ....

....

....

....

The bones that articulate at the knee joint are the ....

....

The movement at position B is flexion in the ....

....

The agonist muscles creating this movement are the ....

The plane of movement that the athlete will move through during the squat is the

....

The agonist muscles will be working eccentrically at position B as they are ....
....

Ankle

The type of joint at the ankle is a ....
....
....
....
....
....
....

The bones that articulate at the ankle joint are ....
....
....
....
....

The movement shown from position A to position B is ....
....
....

The agonist muscle creating this movement is ....
....
....
....
....

The plane of movement ....
....
....
....
....

The tibialis anterior muscles will be working concentrically at ....

....

....

....

....

....

Hip

The type of joint at the hip is ....

....

....

....

....

....

The bones that articulate at the hip joint are the ....

....

....

....

....

....

The movement produced at the hip from position A to position B is ....

....

....

....

....

The agonist muscle creating this movement is the ....

....

....

....

....

The plane of movement that the athlete will move through is the ....

....

....

....

....

The rectus femoris muscles will be contracting concentrically at Position B, enabling ....

....

....

....

....

....

> **Links** To revise the location of bones, see page 79 of the Revision Guide and see pages 85 and 99 for types of joint and movement at them, page 91 for types of contraction, page 93 for location of skeletal muscles, page 96 for antagonistic muscle pairs and pages 97–98 for planes of movement.

Total for Question 12 = 20 marks

END OF PAPER

TOTAL FOR PAPER 1 = 70 MARKS

Revision paper 2

To support your revision, this Workbook contains revision tests to help you revise the skills that might be needed in your exam. Ask your tutor or check the Pearson website for the most up-to-date Sample Assessment Material to get an idea of the structure of your exam and what this requires of you. Details of the actual exam may change so always make sure you are up to date.

Answer ALL questions. Write your answers in the spaces provided.

1 Identify the **two** valves that operate between the atria and the ventricles in the heart. **2 marks**

In **identify** questions, you assess factual information that may require a single word answer, although sometimes a few words or a maximum of a single sentence are required.

1 ....

2 ....

Links See page 67 of the Revision Guide for the anatomy of the heart.

Total for Question 1 = 2 marks

2 a) Name the function of red blood cells. **1 mark**

In **name** questions, you give a definition or an example.

....

....

b) Name the function of platelets. **1 mark**

....

....

Links See page 69 of the Revision Guide to revise the composite parts of blood and their functions.

Total for Question 2 = 2 marks

Unit 2

3 Describe the function of arteries. `2 marks`

....
....
....
....
....

> **Links** See page 68 of the Revision Guide to revise the location and anatomy of blood vessels, including arteries.

Total for Question 3 = 2 marks

4 Explain the function of the chemoreceptors and medulla oblongata during breathing. `4 marks`

....
....
....
....
....
....
....
....
....

> **Links** See page 75 of the Revision Guide to revise neural (medulla oblongata) and chemical (chemoreceptors) control of breathing.

Total for Question 4 = 4 marks

5 Describe the process of bone growth. `3 marks`

....
....
....
....
....

> **Links** See page 77 of the Revision Guide to revise bone growth.

Total for Question 5 = 3 marks

6 Describe the mechanisms of breathing. **5 marks**

....
....
....
....
....
....
....
....

> **Links** See page 73 of the Revision Guide to revise inspiration and expiration.

Total for Question 6 = 5 marks

7 Table 1 shows the change in a footballer's gaseous exchange when taking part in training.

Gas	% in air	% in exhaled air during training	% in exhaled air at rest
O_2	21	17	15
CO_2	0.049	3	6

Table 1

Explain, using Table 1, how gaseous exchange allows the footballer to perform during training. **4 marks**

> When you **explain**, you show your **understanding** by making a statement or point and then **justifying** it.

....
....
....
....
....
....
....
....

> **Links** See page 74 of the Revision Guide to revise gaseous exchange.

Total for Question 7 = 4 marks

Unit 2

8 Chris is a rugby player. When he plays in a rugby match, he will recruit different classifications of joints to enable him to move his body.

Explain why different classifications of joints would be used when Chris plays rugby. **4 marks**

....

....

....

....

....

....

....

....

Links See pages 84 and 85 of the Revision Guide to revise classification of joints and their types.

Total for Question 8 = 4 marks

9 Describe how ligaments support sporting movements at the knee. **4 marks**

....

....

....

....

....

....

....

....

Links See page 83 of the Revision Guide to revise the function of ligaments.

Total for Question 9 = 4 marks

10 Figure 1 shows an athlete taking part in a 100 m sprint.

Figure 1

Assess the action of sprinter's back leg during the sprint shown in Figure 1.

8 marks

> In **assess** questions, you need to present a careful consideration of **varied factors** or **events** that apply to a specific situation. Or you should identify those which are the most **important** or **relevant** to arrive at a **conclusion**.

Links To revise types of joints, see page 85 of the Revision Guide and see page 99 for movements at joints, page 91 for types of muscle contraction, page 93 for the location of skeletal muscles and page 96 for antagonistic muscle pairs.

Total for Question 10 = 8 marks

11 Figure 2 shows an athlete performing squats.

Figure 2

To what extent does the sliding filament theory describe the movement in Figure 2.

12 marks

In **to what extent** questions, you **review** information then bring together a balanced **judgement or conclusion**, giving your **reasons**.

Links See page 90 of the Revision Guide to revise sliding filament theory.

Total for Question 11 = 12 marks

12 Figure 3 shows an athlete performing an overarm throw in basketball.

Figure 3

Analyse the movements at the elbow, shoulder and wrist joints at stages A, B and C which allow the basketball player to throw the ball.

20 marks

> When you are asked to **analyse movements**, you need to break them down into their components, **methodically** and in **detail**.
> **Identify** the separate factors and say how they are related. **Explain** how each one contributes to the movement.
> You could produce a quick **thought plan** or **table** to help you cover the different elements in your answer.

Links See page 79 of the Revision Guide to revise location of bones, pages 85 and 99 to revise types of joint and movement at them, page 91 to revise types of contraction, page 93 to revise location of skeletal muscles and page 96 to revise antagonistic muscle pairs.

Total for Question 12 = 20 marks

END OF PAPER

TOTAL FOR PAPER 2 = 70 MARKS

Unit 3: Applied Sport and Exercise Psychology

Your set task

Unit 3 will be assessed through a task, which will be set by Pearson. You will use your understanding of interpreting psychological factors and applying psychological theories to provide guidance to an individual or team on psychological interventions in response to psychological factors that are impacting on their performance.

Your Revision Workbook

> This Workbook is designed to **revise skills** that might be needed in your assessed task. The selected content, outcomes, questions and answers are provided to help you revise content and ways of applying your skills. Ask your tutor or check the Pearson website for the most up-to-date Sample Assessment Material and Mark Scheme to get an indication of the structure of your actual assessed task and what this requires of you. The detail of the actual assessed task may change so always make sure you are up to date.

To support your revision, this Workbook contains revision activities to help you revise the skills that might be needed in your assessed task.

Revision activities will help you to:
- relate your learning to a sport and exercise context
- consider psychological theories in relation to psychological factors
- consider psychological interventions.

You will then use your work to:
- interpret psychological factors
- apply psychological theories
- recommend psychological interventions.

> **Links** To help you revise skills that might be needed in your Unit 3 assessed task, this Workbook contains revision activities. See the introduction on page iii for more information on features included to help you revise.

Unit 3
Guided

Revision activities

> The revision activities on pages 63–70 are designed to **revise skills** that might be needed in your assessed task. **In your actual task**, the information you are given may be divided into parts and will **differ** from the information in these revision activities. Ask your tutor or check the **Pearson website** for the most up-to-date **Sample Assessment Material** to get an indication of the structure of your assessed task and what this requires of you. Details of the actual assessed task may change so always make sure you are up to date.

Relate your learning to a sports and exercise context

 Read the notes below to get an understanding of an individual and the challenges she experiences as a national team rugby player. This will give you an overview of:
- the **challenges** faced when entering a new team
- **personality changes** between being on field and off field
- what **motivates** her to succeed
- the **impact** of an injury.

Complete the notes on the psychological factors impacting on Emily and possible theories and interventions that might apply.

> Guided

Individual's performance	Psychological factors	Possible theories/interventions
Emily: 23-year-old rugby player; recently selected for the Women's England Rugby Team.	Rugby requires positive aggression to be successful	Bandura's social learning thoery
Loves competing for the country; gets goose bumps every time she puts on an England shirt.	Motivation	Need achievement theory
Known for getting very nervous before a game which at times can show in the first 10 minutes of any match.	Effect of arousal negative in the first 10 minutes.	Inverted ....
After the initial phases of the game Emily transforms into a loud, confident, dominant and aggressive player making tackles all over the pitch.	....	Vealey's Multidimensional model of sport confidence
Relishes the opportunity to beat her opponents	Positive aggression within the laws of the game	Bandura's .... theory
The feeling that she gets from winning helps to motivate her to train harder and supports her as she builds up to the next competition.	.... from her success	Need achievement theory

(Continued on next page)

Unit 3 Guided

Individual's performance	Psychological factors	Possible theories/interventions
In a match, Emily is stretchered off with a serious knee injury requiring immediate surgery to re-attach her anterior cruciate ligament (ACL). The injury is serious and requires a lengthy rehabilitation programme. Emily is convinced she will never play rugby again.	Self-efficacy	Bandura's .... theory
Since being injured, Emily's personality has changed. She has become argumentative and gets frustrated easily. Eight weeks on, Emily has withdrawn from social situations choosing to stay at home.	Learned helplessness	.... theory
She relies on social media to keep up to date with what is going on and sees that her team mates have been selected to participate in the Olympics. Emily is upset, angry and annoyed that nobody told her directly. She talks with her physiotherapist and realises she has withdrawn from her team mates despite them trying to include her.	Hostile aggression	.... social learning theory
Emily realises the significant physiological and psychological effect of the injury, resulting in negative thought processes that prevent her getting better physically. She learns that through hard work she could play rugby again, which improves her outlook on her injury and develops a 'can do' attitude. Sixteen weeks on, Emily returns to training, feeling excited yet nervous about seeing everyone.	Self-efficacy Motivation	....
At training, she discusses her feelings with the coach who suggests she may benefit from some psychology support.		Possible interventions: Positive self-talk .... statements Progressive .... relaxation Breathing .... Imagery .... talks Goal setting .... profiling

Links To revise relevant psychological factors on exercise and performance, see pages 119 and 124–127 of the Revision Guide for motivation, pages 128–130 for arousal, page 138 for aggression, pages 140–141 for self-confidence, page 143 for self-efficacy and page 146 for learned helplessness.

Consider psychological theories in relation to psychological factors

> Complete the notes below on the **psychological theories** applied to the key **psychological factors** on pages 63–64. Make sure you explain and apply your points in relation to the positive and negative impact on Emily's performance. Consider the significance of the impact on performance, and the priorities for Emily.

Theory: Need achievement theory
- Individuals can be categorised into two groups in respect of motivation – the need to achieve and the need to avoid failure.
- Individuals in the need to achieve group tend to strive for success and take a pride in their accomplishments.
- Those in the need to avoid failure group are afraid to fail and avoid challenges and risks.

Psychological factor: Motivation
- High motivation is a key characteristic of successful sports performers, closely linked to arousal.
- Emily's motivation is intrinsic; she is driven by the need to achieve; likes the feeling of winning; sense of achievement is a focus; uses it to help prepare for next match; supports her success during training and matches; affects her ability to perform.
- Optimum level of motivation before over-motivation takes place which can cause injury. Injury affects Emily's motivation negatively; as she realises recovery is possible, motivation returns with a positive impact.

Theory: Inverted U hypothesis
- States that there is an optimum level of arousal to ....
  ....
  ....
- When arousal is ....
  ....
  ....

Psychological factor: Arousal
- Self-regulation of arousal levels is a key characteristic of successful sports performers.
- It is clear that, prior to competing, Emily is in a state of increased arousal, demonstrated by
  ....
- Initially, the level of arousal has a ....
- Then, ...
  ....

Theory: Vealey's multidimensional model of sport confidence
- Suggests that there are key areas that need to be fulfilled to promote self-confidence.
- Factors such as ....
  ....
  ....

Psychological factor: Self-confidence
- High levels of self-confidence are key characteristics of successful sports performers. It is important that Emily is self-confident in rugby due to ....
- Emily displays high confidence ....
  ....
- Significant personality changes seen ....
  ....

Theory: Bandura's social learning theory
- Explains that aggression is a behaviour which is learned by observing others and ....
  ....
- Reinforcement can be from anyone and ....
  ....

Psychological factor: Aggression
- Instrumental, controlled aggression is important for Emily for ....
  ....
- Emily's aggression is suitable, ...

Theory: Bandura's self-efficacy theory
- Suggests that an individual's beliefs about their capabilities to complete a task have a profound effect as to whether they are ....
- The theory explains that there are four sources ....
  ....

Psychological factor: Self-efficacy
- Positive thinking is a key characteristic of successful sports performers. Self-efficacy is closely linked to self confidence.
- Emily's self-efficacy is ....
  ....
  ....
  ....

Theory: Dweck's theory

- Argues that people have either a fixed or growth mindset. A fixed mindset is where ....
....
....

- In contrast, a growth mindset is ....
....

Psychological factor: Learned helplessness

- Emily feels as if she has failed because of the impact of the injury, and experiences ....
....
....

- Dweck's theory suggests that ....
....
....

- To assist Emily in getting better and returning to playing rugby, ...
....

> **Links** To revise application of relevant psychological theories on exercise and performance, see pages 120–123 of the Revision Guide for theories about motivation, pages 128–129 for arousal performance theories, page 139 for theories of aggression, page 140 for Vealey's multidimensional model of sport confidence, page 144 for Bandura's self-efficacy theory and page 146 for Dweck's theory.

Consider psychological interventions

Guided — Complete the thought plan below about the principles behind psychological interventions.

Principles behind psychological interventions:

- Tools to support athletes in ....
- Boosts key characteristics for successful ....
- Specified amount of time to be given as part of the agreement so that ....
- Procedure to be agreed by performer and coach – if there is no agreement ....
- Essential for trustworthy relationship between athlete and ....

Complete the table below which suggests and justifies a range of relevant interventions to help Emily recover from her injury. Add your own thoughts and notes, suggesting what would be a priority for Emily, and why.

Guided

Intervention	How implemented	Justification
Positive self-talk, useful for Emily's: • Learned helplessness • Self-confidence • Arousal • Aggression	Used to produce a .... attitude. Involves statements such as .... It does not use task specific instructions. Cue words or phrases can also be used to help refocus or highlight key elements.	Significant impact on an individual's mind set. It is important that self-talk is used to turn negative thought patterns associated with long-term injuries into positive ones.
Additional notes:		
Positive statements, useful for Emily's: • Learned helplessness • Self-efficacy	Series of phrases or sentences that can be said to an athlete. Statements used are personal to them, short, clear and simple. Emotive words are used	....

Unit 3
Guided

Intervention	How implemented	Justification
Additional notes:		
Goal setting, useful for Emily's: • Learned helplessness • Motivation • Self-confidence	Key component that keeps athlete focused on specific areas for improvement; goals are often categorised into .... highlighting the various durations needed between setting and completing. Short-term goals can bring quick success and increase motivation levels; short and medium-term goals makes progress to	Crucial for final stages of rehabilitation that Emily is focused and positive about moving forward. Can be used to refocus an athlete, concentrating on the here and now or the near future and re-motivate them into achieving, performing and succeeding. Acts as a ....
Additional notes:		
Imagery, useful for Emily's: • Self-efficacy • Arousal • Self confidence • Aggression	Creates pictures in the mind for each individual aspect of a skill, along with the emotions that are commonly felt as part of the activity, without physically completing the skill. Uses visual, auditory and kinaesthetic senses for imagery to be most effective. The principles allow skills to be .... Used to create a growth mindset.	Assists with ....
Pep talks, useful for Emily's self-efficacy	Most effective from people who the athlete has a good relationship with. Emotive language assists the athlete to	Provides a boost to the athlete; designed to create feelings of self-belief.

Unit 3
Guided

Intervention	How implemented	Justification
Additional notes:		
Progressive muscular relaxation (PMR), useful for Emily's: • Arousal • Aggression	....	Avoids increased muscle tension which reduces the flexibility in muscles, creating a decrease in their range of movement; exposure creates awareness of muscle tension; difficult to use PMR during a sporting situation.
Additional notes:		
Breathing control, useful for Emily's: • Arousal • Aggression	Relaxes and restores an athlete to a regular breathing pattern where an athlete is over-aroused/anxious so feeling an increase in perceived pressure within sporting situations which alters their breathing pattern.	....
Additional notes:		
Performance profiling, useful for Emily's motivation	Breaks down requirements of sport and attributes for successful performance, agreed by coach and player. Athlete and coach score athlete on 1–10 scale for how good they think they are with each attribute, then discuss results and major differences. Information is used	Used in final stages of rehabilitation, to increase .... Important that it is included as part of recovery; needs to be executed effectively or it could have a detrimental effect on the anticipated outcome.
Additional notes:		

 **Links** To revise the application of relevant psychological interventions to exercise and performance, see pages 156–166 of the Revision Guide.

Revision questions

> To support your revision, this Workbook contains revision questions to help you **revise the skills** that might be needed in your assessed task. The details of the assessed task may change so always make sure you are up to date. Ask your tutor or check the Pearson website for the most up-to-date Sample Assessment Material to get an idea of the structure of your assessed task and what this requires of you.

Using notes

In this revision workbook, you can refer to any of the notes you have made as you give answers to the questions that follow.

In your actual assessment, you may not be allowed to refer to notes, or there may be restrictions on the length and type of notes that are allowed. Check with your tutor or look at the most up-to-date Sample Assessment Material on the Pearson website to find out what information you might be given about an individual or team, whether the information will be given in parts, and when you will be given the information.

You are required to provide psychological guidance for a client and their performance needs based on the information provided about Emily on pages 63–70 and the questions below.

Revision question 1

Interpret the psychological **factors** that impact on Emily and her performance (see pages 72–76).

Revision question 2

Analyse how psychological **theories** can account for Emily's experiences (see pages 77–81).

Revision question 3

Recommend psychological **interventions** that address Emily's needs.

In your answer, you should justify any recommendations made (see pages 82–88).

Unit 3
Guided

Revision question 1

Interpret the psychological **factors** that impact on Emily and her performance.

Refer to the information about Emily on pages 63–70. Use the guide below to complete your response, which reflects one way of structuring an answer. You need to cover the following points within your answer:
- identify **positive** and **negative** psychological **factors**
- **interpret** the **impact** of psychological factors, demonstrating **relevance** to the individual
- **prioritise** the **significance** of each psychological factor and its **effect** on **performance**.

 You may find it useful to **create a quick thought plan** of key points. Complete the plan below.

Interpreting the psychological factors impacting on Emily's performance

Motivation
- Positive at first
- Negative after injury – high intrinsic motivation knocked
- Returning in recovery – needs to build up

Learned helplessness
- Needs to address as a priority to return to successful rugby
- Positive pre-injury
- ....
- ....
- .... after injury

Self-efficacy
- Needs to restore as a priority to improve
- Negative post-injury, decrease linked with anxiety and fear
- Positive at first
- Negative after the injury
- Needs to improve self-confidence post-injury and not fear returning to team
- ....

Aggression
- Positive, controlled aggression pre-injury
- Negative, hostile agression post-injury, wtih change in mood state
- Needs to return to controlled aggression

....
- Positive pre-injury, though nervous initially
- Needs to regulate levels
- Negative in first 10 minutes, over-aroused, decreased performance
- Positive as game progresses

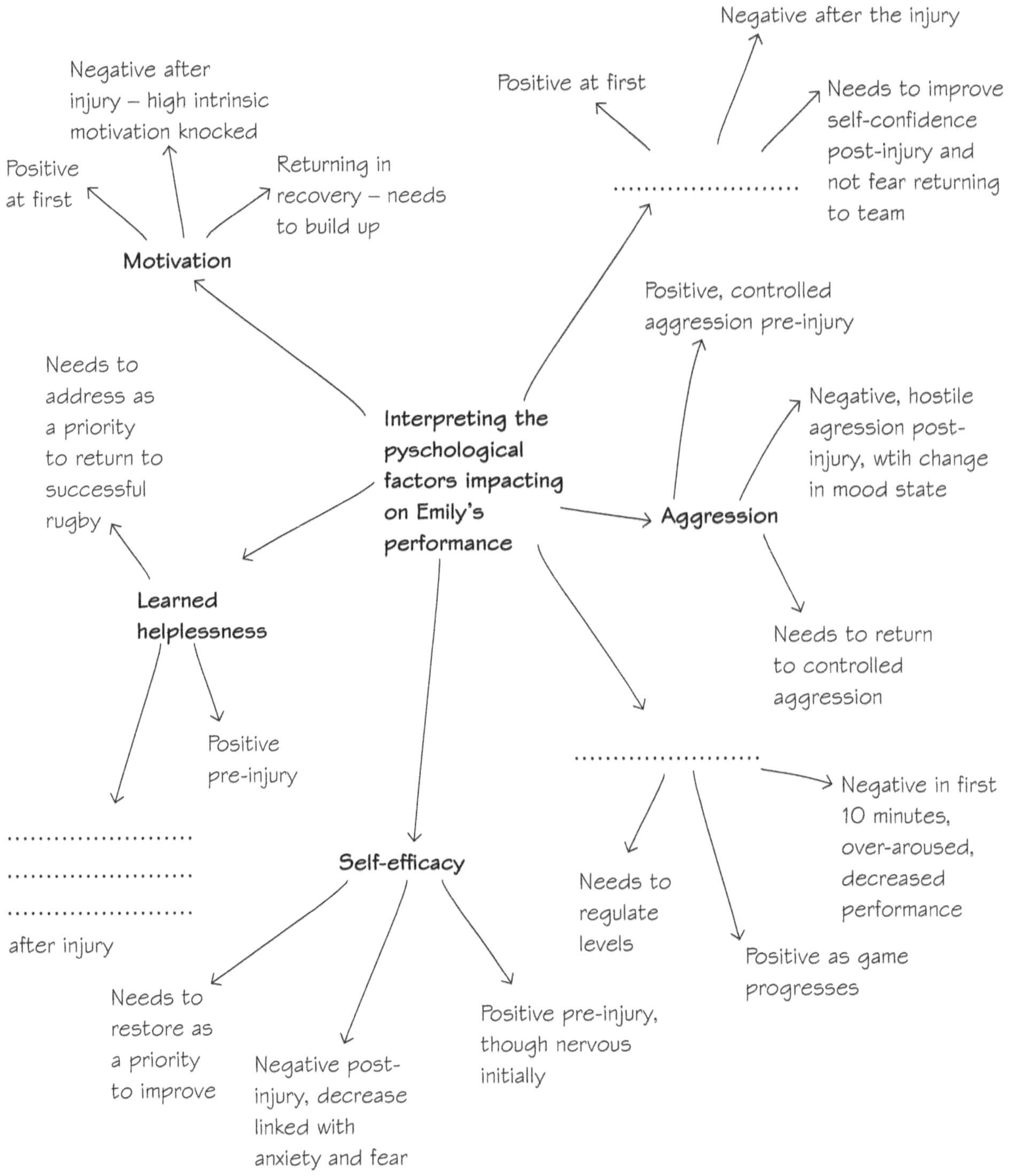

Unit 3
Guided

There are a number of psychological factors which have an effect on Emily's performance, both positively and negatively.

> Start by interpreting the impact of factors that affect Emily positively when she is performing, such as **motivation**. Consider her motivation before the injury, after the injury and then as she prepares to return to training.

Motivation affects Emily's performance positively, with high intrinsic motivation. She is highly motivated as she has achieved a place on the national circuit – a real positive as it is not easy to be selected by your national team. She enjoys the feeling when she wins, with a sense of pride and achievement. As she is intrinsically motivated, winning matches assists her in getting ready for the next match. However, when Emily becomes injured her motivation seems to disappear as she convinces herself that she won't play rugby again. Emily's motivation is low after her injury when she becomes isolated but in her physiotherapy session, where she makes a positive decision to get better and try to join the team, her motivation starts to develop again. Emily's motivation recovers to a position of excitement on returning to the game, although she is nervous. It is essential that Emily is highly motivated so that she can continue ....

....

> Go on to interpret the impact that **self-confidence** has on Emily. Think about the effect before her injury and also how this changes after her injury.

Self-confidence also affects Emily positively prior to her injury. High levels of self-confidence are essential for successful rugby performances, especially to compete with the best in the world. Emily is not afraid to challenge ....

Emily's self-confidence declines when she is injured ....

....

However, physiotherapy leads to ....

....

....

> Next, interpret the impact that **aggression** has on Emily. Think about the effect on her performance before her injury and as she prepares to return to training.

Aggression is also a positive psychological factor for Emily prior to injury. Controlled aggression is

instrumental ....

....

....

This changes after her injury to...

....

....

Emily needs to regain controlled aggression and ....

....

Unit 3
Guided

> Now consider a factor that has a negative impact on Emily's performance when she starts her match – **arousal**. Think about the effect at first, as the match continues and as she prepares to return to training.

Arousal impacts on Emily negatively at the start of the match, as her performance is decreased in the first 10 minutes, before it settles down.

Emily's attentional focus could be ....

....

When returning to training, Emily needs to ....

....

> Next, interpret how the psychological factor of **self-efficacy** impacts on Emily. Think about how it is impacted by the injury and how it develops as she prepares to return to training.

Emily's self-efficacy is strong initially as she ....

....

....

After her injury, ...

....

A turning point takes place ....

....

This leads to ....

> Next, interpret how **learned helplessness** impacts on Emily. Consider how she is affected by learned helplessness following the injury, and her efforts to challenge this factor as she prepares to return to training.

Learned helplessness is having the most significant negative effect on Emily. Initiallly Emily is in a

strong ....

....

After her injury Emily shows a fixed mindset with ....

....

....

....

A change in perception takes place ....

....

....

Unit 3
Guided

> Now **prioritise the significance** of **each psychological factor** in terms of the effect on Emily's performance. Some factors may relate to Emily prior to returning to performance, others may be more short term or future based, as Emily experiences the impact of her injury and recovery. The order will depend on what you believe to be her **priority**. Make sure you **justify** why you have selected this order. Start with **learned helplessness**.

The highest priority for Emily should be reducing the effect that learned helplessness is having on her during her rehabilitation stages. This is because learned helplessness will inhibit Emily's ability to get better. When an athlete an athlete gets injured they will suffer with feelings of anger, frustration and sadness. The impact this has on performance is to delay return to the sport with potential to also reduce exercise. Emily needs to improve her mental wellbeing, complete her rehabilitation exercises and return to playing. By making this a priority, it will assist Emily by empowering her

....

....

> Next consider a further **high** priority. Remember to include a **justification** as to why you believe it should be high priority, saying why it is **significant** with direct **links** to Emily's experiences.

A further high priority should be .... This is because ....

....

....

The impact this has on performance is ....

....

.... By making this a priority, it will assist Emily by ....

....

> Next, consider a **medium** priority:
> – **Why** have you placed it as medium priority?
> – **What impact** will improving it have on Emily and her performance?

A medium priority should be .... This is because ....

....

The impact this has on performance is ....

....

.... By making this a priority, it will assist Emily by ....

....

> Outline a further **medium** priority, giving reasons why it is medium priority. Is it because **improvements** will take **longer**, or is the **impact** of the psychological factor **less** than the others?

A further medium priority should be .... This is because ....

....

....

The impact this has on performance is ....
....
.... By making this a priority, it will assist Emily by ....
....
....

> Outline the final two priorities, which would be **lower** priority. Remember to include your **justification** and outline the **significance** of each psychological factor for Emily.

A lower priority should be ....
....
....
....
....
....

A further lower priority should be ....
....
....
....
....

> Your **conclusion** could sum up which psychological factors are most important for Emily, the ways they have affected her and key priorities for improvement.

In conclusion, it can be argued that there are a number of psychological factors which have a positive and/or negative influence on Emily and her performance in rugby. The impact these factors have on performance varies greatly ....
....
....

The key priorities for improvement and the factors demonstrated as having the most significant effect are ....
....
....

> **Links** To revise relevant psychological factors on exercise and performance, see pages 119 and 124–127 of the Revision Guide for motivation, pages 128–130 for arousal, page 138 for aggression, pages 140–141 for self-confidence, page 143 for self-efficacy, page 146 for learned helplessness and page 171 to revise approaches for responding to this kind of activity.

Revision question 2

Analyse how psychological **theories** can account for Emily's experiences.

> Refer to the information about Emily on pages 63–70. Use the guide below which reflects one way of structuring an answer. You need to cover the following points:
> - show your detailed knowledge of **psychological theories**
> - **apply** psychological theory specifically to each identified **psychological factor**, with supporting **justification**
> - take an **analytical** approach that **links theory to factors** identified about Emily's experiences..

You may also find it useful to use a **brief flow chart** like the one below to ensure you include the **key points** in relation to each psychological factor and theory.

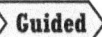 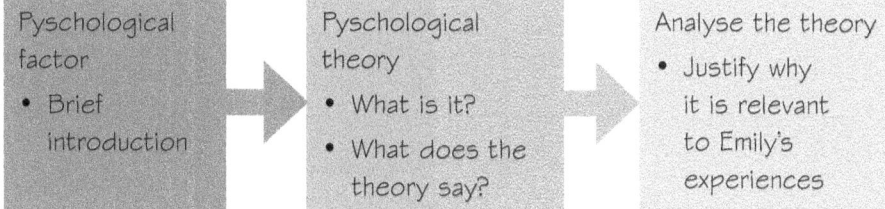

A number of psychological theories link to the psychological factors identified as impacting on Emily both positively and negatively in her experiences.

It is clear that Emily is intrinsically motivated and the level of motivation has a significant impact on her performance. The psychological theory that best accounts for Emily's intrinsic motivation is the need achievement theory. This theory suggests that all athletes can be grouped into two categories – the need to achieve group or the need to avoid failure group. The athletes who need to achieve strive for success and keep going when things go wrong. They feel a sense of pride in their accomplishments.

> This opening identifies the psychological factor of **motivation** and links it with the **need achievement theory** in relation to Emily's performance. The theory is then explained in more detail. Continue by analysing the theory further and justifying its use in Emily's case in relation to the impact of injury and her recovery.

Prior to injury, Emily demonstrates ....

....

....

It is recognised that characteristics of an individual may change in response to a situation, so a 'need to achieve' position may change to a 'need to avoid failure'. In Emily's case, after her injury,

....

....

....

During the recovery phase, the theory will be used to support Emily to a successful return through

....

....

This clearly demonstrates that the need achievement theory is relevant to Emily because ....

....

Unit 3 Guided

> Now identify and explain how **psychological theory links** to Emily's **self-confidence** in her experiences.

Another psychological factor that has influenced Emily and her performance is self-confidence. This is needed because ....

....

A theory that is relevant to Emily's experience is Vealey's multidimensional model of sport confidence. This model explains that ....

....

....

....

....

....

> Go on to **analyse** the theory, **applying** it to Emily's experiences.

It is evident that Vealey's multidimensional model of sport confidence is applicable to Emily's experiences because prior to her injury displays self-confidence but after injury Emily's self-confidence is lowered, resulting in ....

....

....

In recovery, the role of the physiotherapist and psychologist includes emotional support through

....

....

....

> Next identify and explain how **psychological theory links** to Emily's **aggression** in her experiences.

Changes occur in the psychological factor of aggression before and after Emily's injury, changing from instrumental aggression to hostile aggression. Aggression is a key component needed to assist an individual to become successful within the sport. The aggression displayed when playing can be accounted for by Bandura's social learning theory ....

....

....

Unit 3
Guided

> Go on to **analyse** the theory, **applying** it to Emily's different experiences. Comment on the changes seen in aggression with Emily after her injury, from **instrumental aggression** to **hostile aggression** and what is needed in recovery.

Prior to injury, Emily ....

....

After injury, the aggression type changes ....

....

Through the recovery process ....

....

....

> Now identify and explain how **psychological theory links** to Emily's **arousal**.

Arousal can be closely linked to motivation and self-confidence. The effect of arousal on Emily demonstrates the impact of over-arousal on her performance within the first 10 minutes. However, as the match continues the feelings appear to settle down enabling Emily to perform to the best of her ability. This is a classic description of behaviours which relate to the Inverted U hypothesis.

This explains that ....

....

....

....

....

> Go on to **analyse** the theory, **applying** it to Emily's different experiences.

Prior to injury, ...

....

Following the injury and when returning to training, ...

....

....

This theory can be applied in the recovery process as Emily pushes herself to get better. However, this must be carefully managed to ensure ....

....

....

Unit 3
Guided

> Next identify and explain how **psychological theory links** to Emily's **self-efficacy** in her experiences.

Self-efficacy is ....

The theory that relates to this is ....

.... The theory explains that ....

....

....

....

....

....

> Go on to **analyse** Bandura's self-efficacy theory, **applying** it to Emily's experiences.

To demonstrate how this theory applies to Emily, it is useful to look at her situation before and after her injury, and as she recovers. At first, ...

....

....

....

....

....

....

> Next identify and explain how **psychological theory links** to Emily's **learned helplessness**.

....

....

....

....

....

....

....

> Go on to **analyse** Dweck's theory of learned helplessness, **applying** it to Emily's experiences.

....

....

....

....

....

....

....

....

> Your **conclusion** could sum up **key factors** that will lead into proposed interventions.

In conclusion, it is clear that a number of different psychological theories can be applied to the psychological factors impacting on Emily and her performance. The importance of Emily responding

positively ....

....

....

> **Links** To revise application of relevant psychological theories on exercise and performance, see pages 120–123 of the Revision Guide for theories about motivation, pages 128–129 for arousal performance theories, page 139 for theories of aggression, page 140 for Vealey's multidimensional model of sport confidence, page 144 for Bandura's self-efficacy theory, page 146 for Dweck's theory and page 172 to revise approaches for responding to this kind of activity.

Unit 3 Guided

Revision question 3

Recommend psychological **interventions** to address Emily's needs. In your answer you should justify any recommendations made.

> Refer to the information about Emily on pages 63–70. Use the guide below to complete the answer, which reflects one way of structuring an answer. You need to cover the following points within your answer:
> - show your detailed knowledge of **principles** behind psychological interventions
> - select psychological interventions that are **relevant** to Emily and each identified psychological factor that requires intervention
> - provide a detailed **justification** for the interventions selected, showing clear **application** to Emily's needs and priorities.

 You may find a brief **flowchart** like the one below useful to ensure you include the key points in relation to each psychological intervention.

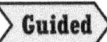

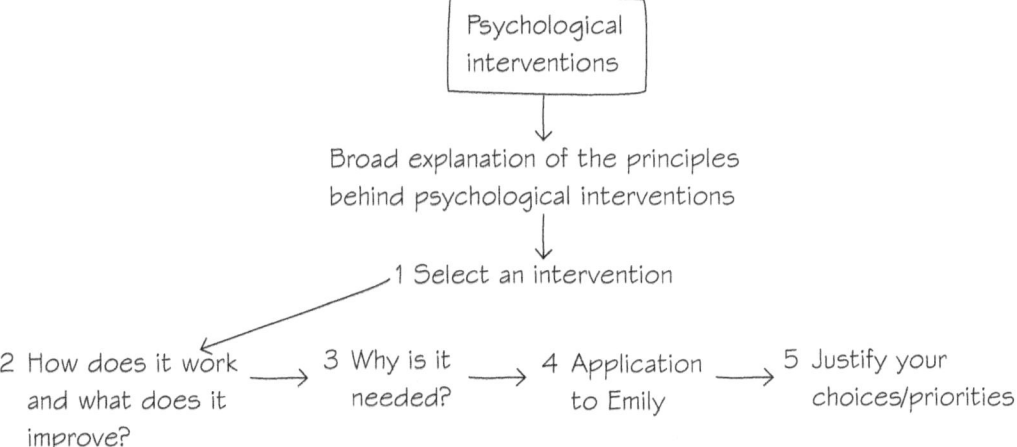

> The opening of this answer states what **psychological interventions** are. It is important to show detailed knowledge of the principles surrounding psychological interventions.

Psychological interventions are tools to support athletes in aspects of performance. A number of interventions could be used to enhance Emily's state of mind and her performance in relation to the identified psychological factors following her injury.

For psychological interventions to be successful, a number of principles need to be fulfilled. First, there should be a trustworthy relationship between the athlete and the person implementing the intervention. This is essential if the intervention is to be successful. Second, the procedure should be agreed by the performer and the coach. If there is no agreement, the intervention should not take place. Third, it is recommended that, as part of the agreement, a specified amount of time is given so that all parties ....

> Go on to recommend **interventions** for the identified psychological factors, to meet Emily's needs and priorities. Start by recommending **self-talk** for Emily.

Self-talk involves talking to oneself in a positive manner about themselves. It is commonly non-verbal dialogue. The process involves changing negative thoughts ....

....

....

It is needed to assist Emily in relation to improving the impact of psychological factors of ....
....

Following the injury, this intervention could become part of Emily's immediate rehabilitation progress.

She could ....

....

....

....

Having built in self-talk to support Emily with her rehabilitation it could then be transferred ....

....

....

....

This is a high priority for Emily because it will enable her to ....

....

....

....

....

....

> Next move on to recommend **goal setting** as an intervention.

Goal setting is used to assist an athlete to remain focused. Goals are categorised into short, medium and long term, and it is important to agree the timeline between setting them and completing them. Goal setting is needed as a useful intervention to assist Emily with her rehabilitation programme and her return to the team, starting with short-term goals.

It could be used to assist Emily in relation to the psychological factors of ....

....

....

....

....

In Emily's case, goal setting is crucial to enable her to see improvements ....

....

....

To implement goal setting, Emily would need ....

....

Unit 3
Guided

Goal setting is a high priority for Emily and works best for athletes who are intrinsically motivated

....

....

....

....

....

> Now recommend why **positive statements** would be a useful intervention for Emily.

Positive statements can be read by or said to an athlete. As a process changes, so too can the statements in order to reflect the changed situation. The statements are individual to the athlete and ....

....

....

....

They are needed to assist Emily in relation to the psychological factors of ....

....

It is clear that following her injury Emily has got into a cycle of negative thought processes. Positive statements ....

....

....

....

Positive statements are quick to use and ....

....

....

....

This is a high priority for Emily because ....

....

....

> Next recommend why **imagery** would be a useful intervention for Emily.

Imagery involves creating an image or series of images ....

....

....

....

84

....

....

....

It is needed to assist Emily in relation to the psychological factors of ....

....

This tool will especially help to ....

....

Imagery is a skill that can take a while to master correctly. Therefore, ...

....

....

....

This is a high priority for Emily because ....

....

....

> Go on to recommend **pep talks** as a useful intervention for Emily.

A further measure which can be used is pep talks. These are most effective when ....

....

....

....

....

In relation to psychological factors, pep talks are needed to improve ....

....

Pep talks can be used regularly for a significant impact ....

....

Pep talks are a high priority for Emily because ....

....

....

Unit 3
Guided

> Now recommend the intervention of **progressive muscular relaxation (PMR)** for Emily.

Progressive muscular relaxation is used commonly as a relaxation tool. The process ....

....

....

....

....

It is needed to assist Emily in relation to the psychological factors of ....

....

PMR could be used to ....

....

When implementing, PMR is a useful tool ....

....

This is a lower priority overall for Emily at this stage, as ....

....

....

....

....

....

> Next recommend **breathing control** as a useful intervention for Emily.

Breathing control is an intervention that helps the athlete ....

....

....

....

It is needed to assist Emily in relation to the psychological factors of ....

....

This technique is a useful tool that can be applied to Emily to control ....

....

It could be used at any point as it is ....
....
....
....

This is a lower overall priority for Emily because ....
....
....

> Now recommend the intervention of **performance profiling** for Emily.

Performance profiling is a technique used ....
....
....
....
....
....

In relation to psychological factors, it is needed to enhance Emily's ....
....

Performance profiling is a useful tool for someone who is returning ....
....
....

The return from injury is a good time to do this because ....
....
....

This is a lower overall priority for Emily because ....
....
....

Unit 3 Guided

> Your **conclusion** could sum up the most important interventions for the psychological factors that affect Emily following her injury and as she prepares to return to training and performance, to ensure a successful recovery.

In conclusion, a number of interventions are recommended for use by Emily and her coach to assist her in returning from injury, recovering mentally and enhancing her performance. The outline of interventions demonstrates the impact they would have on Emily as an individual and on her performance.

The key findings suggest that priority interventions are ....

....

....

....

....

....

....

Links To revise application of relevant psychological interventions to exercise and performance, see pages 156–166 of the Revision Guide and see page 173 to revise approaches for responding to this kind of activity.

END OF TASK

Unit 13: Nutrition for Sport and Exercise Performance

Your set task

Unit 13 will be assessed through a task, which will be set by Pearson. You will focus on an individual who requires guidance on nutrition in response to their personal and training needs that are impacting on their performance. You will be assessed on your ability to interpret, modify and recommend a nutritional programme for the individual.

Your Revision Workbook

> This Workbook is designed to revise skills that might be needed in your assessed task. The selected content, outcomes, questions and answers are provided to help you revise content and ways of applying your skills. Ask your tutor or check the Pearson website for the most up-to-date Sample Assessment Material and Mark Scheme to get an indication of the structure of your actual assessed task and what this requires of you. The detail of the actual assessed task may change so always make sure you are up to date.

To support your revision, this Workbook contains revision activities to help you revise the skills that might be needed in your assessed task.

The revision activities will help you to relate your learning to a sports and exercise context and revise your understanding of nutrition for health and wellbeing, modifications in relation to sporting events and recommendations in relation to phases of training.

You will then use your work as you:
- interpret an individual's current nutritional programme, in relation to nutritional intake for health and wellbeing
- modify the nutritional programme, based on nutritional strategies, in relation to the individual's sports event
- recommend nutritional guidance for the individual based on their phase of training.

> **Links** To help you revise skills that might be needed in your Unit 13 assessed task, this Workbook contains revision activities. See the introduction on page iii for more information on features included to help you revise.

Revision activities

> The revision activities on pages 90–106 are designed to **revise skills** that might be needed in your assessed task. **In your actual task,** the information you are given may be divided into parts and will **differ** from the information in these revision activities. Ask your tutor or check the **Pearson website** for the most up-to-date **Sample Assessment Material** to get an indication of the structure of your assessed task and what this requires of you. Details of the actual assessed task may change so always make sure you are up to date.

Relate your learning to a sports and exercise context

> Read Olivia's **current nutritional programme** on pages 90–91, then answer the questions that follow.

Olivia's current nutritional programme
MONDAY
Breakfast 7–8am: 1 small glass of orange juice; 1 small serving of porridge made with semi-skimmed milk
Lunch 12–1pm: Baked beans with a sprinkling of grated cheese on two thick slices of wholemeal toast spread lightly with butter
Dinner 6–7pm: Leek and potato soup and a slice of white bread; chicken burger with chips and salad
Fluids throughout the day: 2 mugs of tea; 1 glass of water
Snacks throughout the day: 1 satsuma; 1 large chocolate chip cookie
Energy (calories): 2265; **Fluid (ml):** 1255; **Macronutrients (g):** CHO: 285; FAT: 85; PRO: 90
TUESDAY
Breakfast 7–8am: 1 small glass of orange juice; 1 small serving of porridge made with semi-skimmed milk
Lunch 12–1pm: Ham and salad sandwich; 1 small piece of chocolate cake; 1 orange
Dinner 6–7pm: Beef lasagne with chips and salad
Fluids throughout the day: 1 mug of tea; 1 x 330 ml bottle of vanilla milkshake; 2 glasses of water; 1.5l bottle of water
Snacks throughout the day: 1 cereal bar
Energy (calories): 3090; **Fluid (ml):** 3955; **Macronutrients (g):** CHO: 370; FAT: 130; PRO: 110
WEDNESDAY
Breakfast 7–8am: 1 small glass of orange juice; 1 small serving of porridge made with semi-skimmed milk
Lunch 12–1pm: Tuna mayonnaise bap; 1 small jacket potato; 1 small slice of coffee and walnut cake; 1 orange
Dinner 6–7pm: Chicken and leek pasta in a creamy sauce with sprinkling of cheese and mixed salad; 1 slice of garlic bread; chocolate fudge cake and ice cream
Fluids throughout the day: 1 mug of tea; 2 glasses of fruit squash
Snacks throughout the day: 1 apple; 1 cereal bar
Energy (calories): 2630; **Fluid (ml):** 1490; **Macronutrients (g):** CHO: 345; FAT: 90; PRO: 110

Olivia's current nutritional programme
THURSDAY
Breakfast 7–8am: 1 small glass of orange juice; 1 small serving of porridge made with semi-skimmed milk; 1 banana; 1 probiotic yogurt
Lunch 12–1pm: Ham and cheese salad sandwich; 1 cereal bar; 1 orange
Dinner 6–7pm: 1 salmon en croute, roasted potatoes and salad
Fluids throughout the day: 1 glass of water
Snacks throughout the day: 1 apple; 1 cereal bar; 1 small bar of chocolate; 1 small bowl of cereal
Energy (calories): 2740; **Fluid (ml):** 1100; **Macronutrients (g):** CHO: 385; FAT: 100; PRO: 75
FRIDAY
Breakfast 7–8am: 1 small glass of orange juice; 1 small serving of porridge made with semi-skimmed milk; 1 satsuma
Lunch 12–1pm: Chicken sandwich; 1 small piece of chocolate cake; 1 orange
Dinner 6–7pm: Macaroni cheese with ham, smoked bacon and onion
Fluids throughout the day: 1 mug of coffee; 1 × 330ml bottle of vanilla milkshake; 1.75l bottle of water
Snacks throughout the day: 2 bananas; 1 small bar of chocolate; 1 cereal bar
Energy (calories): 2180; **Fluid (ml):** 3110; **Macronutrients (g):** CHO: 275; FAT: 80; PRO: 90
SATURDAY
Breakfast 7–8am: 1 small glass of orange juice; 1 small serving of porridge made with semi-skimmed milk; 1 apple
Lunch 12–1pm: Tuna mayonnaise sandwich; 1 banana; 1 low fat yogurt
Dinner 6–7pm: Pork casserole, peas, carrots and mashed potato
Fluids throughout the day: 1 glass of water; 1 mug of coffee; 1.5l bottle of water
Snacks throughout the day: 1 cereal bar; 1 white chocolate cookie; 1 small bar of chocolate; 1 small bowl of cereal with semi-skimmed milk
Energy (calories): 2340; **Fluid (ml):** 3050; **Macronutrients (g):** CHO: 310; FAT: 80; PRO: 95
SUNDAY
Breakfast 7–8am: 1 small glass of orange juice; 1 small serving of porridge made with semi-skimmed milk; 1 apple
Lunch 12–1pm: Tuna mayonnaise sandwich; 1 banana
Dinner 6–7pm: Chicken pie, 1 large jacket potato, carrots, parsnip and spring cabbage
Fluids throughout the day: 1 mug of tea; 1 × 330ml bottle of vanilla milkshake; 1.75l bottle of water
Snacks throughout the day: 1 flapjack; 1 small bowl of cereal with semi-skimmed milk
Energy (calories): 2590; **Fluid (ml):** 2725; **Macronutrients (g):** CHO: 360; FAT: 90; PRO: 85

Answer the following questions about the nutritional programme above, in relation to food and fluid intake for health and wellbeing

1 What do you notice about the variety of Olivia's food and fluid intake?

....

2 What do you notice about Olivia's breakfast choices?

....

3 What do you think about the quality of the snacks?

....

4 What do you think about the fluids consumed?

....

5 Fluid and fat intakes are highest on Tuesday. What is likely to have influenced this?

....

6 Fluid intake is lowest on Thursday and carbohydrate is highest. What is likely to have influenced this?

....

7 Are any sports food or supplements included in the nutritional programme?

....

8 What would you like to investigate further in relation to the intake in the nutritional programme?

....

....

....

Now read Olivia's personal and performance details, along with the current training programme. Then answer the questions that follow on page 93.

Personal details

Olivia is training for a sports event. Her nutritional programme (pages 90–91) represents what she typically consumes during a 7-day period. She is 4 weeks away from taking part in the sports event.

Age	18 years old
Gender	Female
Height	1m 68cm
Weight	57 kg
BIA	20%
Activity levels	High

The low body weight and low body fat suggest that the individual is an endurance athlete.

Performance details

Sporting event: Olivia is training for a National Cross Country Championship over a 6 km distance.

Time of event: It will take place on a Sunday at 11am.

Phase of training: Olivia is in the 'pre-event' phase.

Training currently undertaken and at what time of day

Monday: 40-minute run at 10.30am

Tuesday: Warm up and drills; 3 × 1000 m track session at 7.30pm

Wednesday: 45-minute easy run at 4pm

Thursday and Friday: Rest days

Saturday: Speed, agility and balance training at 10.30 am; Hill session; Warm up and drills followed by three sets of 3 × 1-minute hill efforts with 30 seconds to recover; 2–3 mins between sets, at 2pm

Sunday: 30-minute gentle run at 7am; 60-minute run at 4pm

Answer the questions below about Olivia's personal and performance details on page 92 in relation to her current nutritional programme on pages 90–91.

1 What do you notice about the timing of intake in relation to training on Monday?

....

....

....

2 What do you think about the fluid intake on Monday, given it is a training day?

....

3 How are the training sessions on Tuesday reflected in the intake for energy and fluid requirements?

....

....

4 What do you think about the fluid intake on Thursday, given it is a rest day?

....

5 How far has intake on Friday helped prepare for the double training session on Saturday?

....

....

6 Saturday is a double session training day. What do you think about the energy, carbohydrate and fluid intake in relation to this?

....

....

7 Sunday is a double session training day. What do you think about the carbohydrate intake in relation to this?

....

....

8 What implications does the start time for the race have on nutritional preparation for the event?

....

....

Unit 13

Nutrition for health and wellbeing

Complete the revision activities below to be sure that you:
- know the principles of the Eatwell Guide for health and wellbeing
- can use and apply calculations to estimate energy, macronutrient and fluid requirements
- understand the factors that affect digestion and absorption of nutrients and fluids.

 Complete the thought plan below on key Eatwell Guide recommendations for **health** and **wellbeing**.

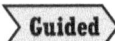

2 Eat plenty of foods rich in
.... and ....

1 Eat the correct amount to maintain a healthy ....

3 Cut back on fat intake particularly that from
....

Eating for health and wellbeing following the Eatwell Guide

4 Ensure adequate intakes of .... and .... by eating a wide variety of foods

6 Do not eat sugary foods too often

5 Keep within sensible limits for alcohol intake

 To estimate **energy** requirements you need to calculate **basal metabolic rate** and then apply a **physical activity level**. Complete the notes below.

Estimating energy requirements

The Harris-Benedict equation for calculating BMR is:

Males: 66.5 + (13.75 × weight in kg) + (5.0 × height in cm) − (6.76 × age in years)

Females: 655.1 + (9.56 × weight in kg) + (1.85 × height in cm) − (4.68 × age in years)

Example 1: female calculation of energy requirements

An 18-year old female athlete weighs 55 kg and is 175 cm tall.

655.1 + (9.56 × 55 kg) + (1.85 × 175 cm) − (4.68 × 18 years)

= 1420 calories

Example 2: male calculation of energy requirements (your own choice of age, weight and height)

A ....-year-old male athlete weighs .... and is .... tall.

....

= .... calories

To predict daily energy requirements, a physical activity level (PAL) needs to be applied. The Harris-Benedict equation recommends the following PAL values to enable calculation of an individual's daily total energy requirement (TER) to maintain current weight.

Physical activity levels (PALS)

- Little to no exercise: TER = BMR × 1.2
- Light exercise (1–3 days a week): TER = BMR × 1.375
- Moderate exercise (3–5 days per week): TER = BMR × 1.55
- Heavy exercise (6–7 days per week): TER = BMR × 1.725
- Very heavy exercise (twice per day, extra heavy workouts): TER = BMR × 1.9

Example 1 of PALS (female calculation of PALS)

A female athlete aged 18 has a BMR of 1436.58 kcal and her activity level is classed as heavy.

To estimate her total daily energy requirement a physical activity factor should be applied of 1.725 giving her a total daily energy requirement of:

1436.58 × 1.725 = 2478 kcal (rounded to the nearest whole number)

Example 2 of PALS (your own choice of age and BMR)

A male athlete aged .... has a BMR of .... and his activity level is classed as very heavy.

To estimate his total daily energy requirement a physical activity factor should be applied of

.... giving him a total daily energy requirement of:

.... × .... = ...

Interpreting Olivia's energy intake from the nutrition programme

- The range of energy intake shown is ....

- The intake might fluctuate to match the needs of her training schedule – the lowest days are

  .... The higher days are ....

- Her average daily intake, adding all values up and dividing by 7 is .... kcal.

 For a more detailed interpretation of Olivia's food intake you will also need to estimate the **macronutrient** requirements. Complete the notes below, starting with **carbohydrates**.

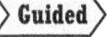 Estimating carbohydrate requirements

To support performance and health, it's recommended that:

- around 50–60 per cent of the total daily calorie intake is derived from carbohydrates
- if athletes are involved in regular intense training, greater intakes may be required (e.g. marathon runners or triathletes may need 65–70 per cent of total daily energy from carbohydrates).

Carbohydrate requirements based on daily activity levels

Level of daily activity	Carbohydrate per kilogram of body weight (g)
Sedentary	3–4
Less than 1 hour	4–5
1 hour	5–6
1–2 hours	6–7
2–3 hours	7–8
More than 3 hours	8–10

Interpreting Olivia's carbohydrate intake from the nutrition programme

- Calculating Olivia's carbohydrate intake over the seven days, her average daily carbohydrate intake is .... g.

- The range of intakes is from .... to .... g.

 Now consider **protein** requirements.

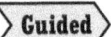 Estimating protein requirements for different sport scenarios

Protein should represent between 12 and 15 per cent of the total energy intake. Nutrition experts do not generally recommend intake beyond 2 g per kg of body weight.

Daily protein requirements based on type of activity

Type of activity	Protein per kg of body weight (g)
Mainly endurance	.... to ....
Mainly strength	.... to ....

Interpreting Olivia's protein intake from the nutrition programme

Olivia's protein intake ranges from .... to .... g.

 Next consider **fat** requirements.

Estimating fat requirements

To support performance and health, the recommendations are as follows.

- Fat intake represents around 30–35 per cent of total calorie intake: around 70 g per day for females and around 90 g per day for males.
- Of this, only 6–10 per cent should be from saturated fats.
- Athletes involved in regular intense activity may need to further reduce overall fat intake as a percentage to around 25–30 per cent of total energy consumed to achieve adequate carbohydrate intakes. However, they will be eating more calories to meet their increased energy requirements, so in absolute terms this may equate to the same quantity of intake as that of a sedentary individual.

Interpreting Olivia's fat intake from the nutrition programme

- In considering Olivia's fat intake her range of intake, is from .... to .... g, with an average intake of .... g per day.

- This is .... the guidelines for the sedentary population for females.

> Now consider **calcium** and **iron** intake. Identify rich sources of these in the current intake.

Interpreting Olivia's calcium and iron intake from the nutrition programme

As a female athlete, Olivia should be encouraged to consume an adequate calcium and iron intake.

In the current intake, rich sources of these are ....

....

> Next evaluate the **fluid** intake with specific reference to the requirements for health and wellbeing.

Estimating fluid requirements

Fluid requirements can be calculated by using either of the following formulae:

A. 30–35 ml per kilogram of body weight per day OR

B. 1 ml per calorie of energy requirement.

Example: fluid requirements for an athlete weighing 57 kg

Using formula A:

.... × .... = ... ml

.... × .... = ... ml

Using formula B:

.... ml per calorie of energy requirement would be .... ml.

Interpreting Olivia's fluid intake from the nutrition programme

- I can see from Olivia's current nutritional intake that her fluid intake is quite inconsistent ranging from .... to .... ml. It would be useful to consider what might be impacting on that.

- When evaluating details of her training programme, her high intake days can be .... her expenditure.

- Her average intake is .... ml per day.

- In assessing the adequacy of Olivia's fluid intake, it would also be helpful to consider the quality of her fluid choices and that she is likely to need ....

....

Unit 13
Guided

> Now move on to evaluate the nutritional programme with specific reference to factors affecting **digestion** and **absorption** of nutrients and fluids.

Guided Interpreting Olivia's nutritional programme with reference to digestion and absorption

Before the body can make use of the energy and nutrients that food contains, it has to be broken down through the processes of digestion and absorption. The precise timing of this depends upon the food which has been eaten and the complexity of its structure. This also varies from person to person, but overall:

- it usually takes 6–8 hours for food to pass through the .... and ....
- .... are digested quickest
- .... takes a bit longer
- .... takes the longest
- slowed by a .... content.

Olivia might want to consider the quantity and type of foods and fluids to consume before, during and after exercise to optimise her nutritional strategies around her sport and exercise. This will be affected by the event she is training for and the days on which she trains.

> Assess Olivia's average intake for **energy**, **fluid** and **macronutrients** over the seven-day period. You can make reference to the Eatwell Guide for health and wellbeing. As you do so, consider:
> - Are some days better than others in meeting predicted requirements?
> - What do you think might be influencing factors on whether requirements are met or not?
> - What do you think might be the outcome of whether requirements are met or not?

Guided Overview of nutrition programme

The Eatwell Guide shows the different types of foods and drinks individuals should consume and in what proportions to obtain a healthy, balanced diet. In order to eat in line with the Eatwell Guide, Olivia should aim to:

- Eat at least .... of fruit and vegetables every day. Olivia eats .... servings per day.

- Base her meals on ....
  She should choose wholegrain versions where possible. Olivia achieves this at her main meals and sometimes uses breakfast cereals as a snack.

- Have some dairy or dairy alternatives, choosing lower .... options where possible. Olivia consumes between .... and .... servings per day.

- Eat some beans, pulses, eggs, meat and other proteins (including two portions of fish every week, and at least one .... fish).

- Choose unsaturated oils and spreads and consume these in .... amounts. It is difficult to tell from Olivia's nutritional programme what types of spreads and oils she uses but some of her snack food choices will be high in fat that might be limiting her overall carbohydrate intake.

- Drink at least .... cups/glasses of fluid a day. Olivia's nutritional programme shows low fluid intakes on at least four days out of the seven. It would need to be explored whether this is a reflection of her actual intake or whether she has just forgotten to record it.

For health, where foods and drinks high in fat, salt or sugar are consumed she have these less often and in small amounts, or restrict ....

....

....

Factors that might be influencing whether Olivia meets her requirements or not could be related to her nutritional knowledge, the time she has to prepare and eat her food in relation to the time she spends training, where she is when she is eating and the food choices available. If she is not meeting her requirements, she is likely to find training harder and recovery from training less than optimal.

> **Links** To revise calculating requirements and interpreting intake relevant to health and wellbeing, see page 176 of the Revision Guide for Recommended Daily Allowance, pages 180–187 for macronutrients, micronutrients and fibre, pages 188–189 for fluids, pages 194–198 for intake for health and wellbeing, pages 201–208 for supplements and sports foods.

Unit 13
Guided

Modifying nutrition for sporting events

Complete the revision activities below to be sure that you:
- can assess the relationship between nutrition intake and training needs
- can optimise a nutritional programme for different situations and apply **nutritional strategies** for **different** sports events and environments
- can target outcomes from suggested modifications whatever the nature of the event.

Complete the thought plan with the information you have about Olivia's nutrition intake and days where nutrition intake is needed for training.

Guided

On Tuesday and Sunday, Olivia has milkshake which links to training days and can be used as

....

....

Information on nutrition intake that may inform nutritional modifications

It would be useful to review the quality of Olivia's snacks and when she consumes them. It might be useful to consider

introducing ....

....

....

The Eatwell Guide provides a good platform for developing sound nutritional strategies for sports performance. Adapt the model to meet the needs of different levels of training demands, so that you optimise the nutritional programme. For example, consider for high demands, using sugary foods to facilitate glycogen recovery after intense training, or being aware that eating lots of high fibre foods might affect appetite and achievement of overall energy requirements.

Optimising the nutritional programme

....

....

....

....

....

....

....

....

....

....

....

....

....

....

Unit 13
Guided

....
....
....
....
....

Understanding key terms
- When you **modify** nutrition intake, you make partial or minor changes to it.
- When you **adapt** nutrition, you make an alteration to it.
- When you propose **strategies** for nutrition, you put forward a method or plan to bring about a desired outcome, such as the achievement of a goal or a solution to a problem.
- When you give **guidance** on nutrition, you give advice or information aimed at resolving or improving something.
- When **recommending** nutrition modifications and strategies, you are putting forward something with approval as being suitable for a particular person, role or situation.
- When **justifying** or **rationalising** proposed nutrition modifications and strategies, you are giving reasons or evidence to:
  - support an opinion and/or decision
  - prove something right or reasonable.

  Complete a **thought plan** of the categories you would need to consider for nutritional modifications and strategies in relation to sporting events.

> Guided

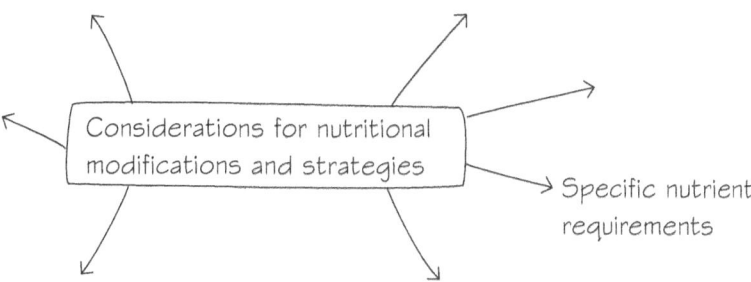

  Complete a **thought plan** of what you expect to be the anticipated outcomes of possible modifications.

> Guided

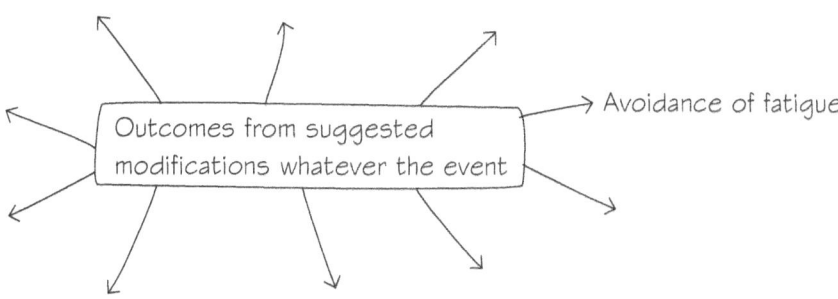

101

Unit 13 Guided

> Develop a day's menu plan to show how you would suggest a nutritional programme could be adapted to support optimal performance in training for some selected training events. Make specific recommendations as appetite and thirst are not always good indicators of energy and fluid needs, and athletes need to benefit from personalised eating and drinking plans.

> **Links** To revise modifications and recommendations, see pages 174–179 of the Revision Guide for nutritional principles, pages 190–193 to revise digestion, absorption and control, pages 194–198 to revise nutritional intake for health and wellbeing, pages 208–211 for nutritional strategies and page 218 for modifying a nutritional programme.

Nutrition intake for different phases of events

Complete the revision activities below to be sure that you can recommend:
- **eating and drinking plans** that are relevant for different **phases** of **sports events** and **environments**
- **pre-event**, **during-event** and **post-event** meal and recovery **strategies**.

A **phase of event** is a distinct stage of a sporting event.

 Complete the thought plans below on nutrition to meet the needs of different phases.

Guidance on nutrition intake for different phases of training and sports events

1 A pre-competition meal should aim to ....

2 Larger meals take longer to digest and nervousness can result in ....

Pre-training or event

4 Competition is not a time to experiment with ....

3 Olivia should be encouraged to begin fully hydrating and to consume fluids ....

Drinking .... to .... ml of fluid .... to .... minutes before exercise is recommended.

Unit 13
Guided

During training or event

1 Fluid loss is a major consideration.

2 During intense training or competition isotonic ....
....
....

3 During endurance or ultra-endurance, events lasting longer than 4 hours
....
....
....

4 Drinking .... to .... ml every .... to .... minutes during exercise is recommended, especially if the exercise lasts longer than an hour

5 Nutritional challenges during the sporting event will likely relate to
....
....
....

Post-training or event

1 Refuel as soon as possible after ....
....
....

2 A high carbohydrate diet ....
....
....

3 Carbohydrates are preferred that are easy to ....

4 Consume a high-carbohydrate (at least .... g) ....
....
....
....
....

5 Rehydration should start immediately. Drinks containing carbohydrates will also assist with ....
....
....
....
....

6 Weight and urine-colour checks are a useful and simple way of monitoring fluid status. weight reduction of .... kg is equivalent to .... of fluid loss.

7 Fluid losses should be replaced ....
....
....

Unit 13
Guided

> Now complete the spidergrams below focusing on:
> - **pre-**, **during** and **post-** training and event **strategies** that can be adapted to suit different sport and event situations
> - the use of **sports foods** and **supplements** and ways in which these might be relevant.

Guided — Nutritional strategies for different sports and phases – factors to consider

Endurance events:

1 Endurance events challenge ....

2 Endurance athletes should aim to maximise glycogen stores by increasing ....

3 Carbohydrate supplements ....

4 Endurance athletes should start exercise ....

5 The longer the duration of the activity, the more important it is to ....

6 Sports drinks can provide ....

Strength and power events:

1 Nutritional strategies should support the development and maintenance of ....

2 Carbohydrate requirements ....

3 Combining carbohydrate with protein post-exercise promotes ....

Weight-category or weight-controlled events:

1 Fewer calories consumed means fewer nutrients consumed

2 Calcium and iron intakes ....

3 Healthy eating and Eatwell Guide principles apply to the planning of dietary intakes for these sports, but greater emphasis may be placed on ....

4 Adequate fluid intake and hydration are essential to maintain ....

105

Unit 13 Guided

<u>Observations for Olivia</u>

- Olivia does not currently consume any ....
- It would be useful to consider the risks versus benefits of any sports foods or supplements that could be incorporated to Olivia's nutritional strategies pre-, during and post- training or during her event. Olivia could consider using ....

....

 **Links** To revise modifications and recommendations, see pages 198–206 and 209–211 of the Revision Guide and to revise application of relevant phase of training intake, see pages 219–220.

Revision questions

> To support your revision, this Workbook contains revision questions to help you revise the skills that might be needed in your assessed task. The details of the assessed task may change so always make sure you are up to date. Ask your tutor or check the Pearson website for the most up-to-date Sample Assessment Material to get an idea of the structure of your assessed task and what this requires of you.

Using notes

In this revision workbook, you can refer to any of the notes you have made as you give answers to the questions that follow.

In your actual assessment, you may not be allowed to refer to notes, or there may be restrictions on the length and type of notes that are allowed. Check with your tutor or look at the most up-to-date Sample Assessment Material on the Pearson website to find out what information you might be given about an individual, whether the information will be given in parts, and when you will be given the information.

Revision question 1

Interpret Olivia's current nutritional programme, in relation to nutritional intake for health and wellbeing.

> Refer to the information about Olivia on pages 90–92. Use the guide below to complete the answer, which reflects one way of structuring a response. You should give:
> - a detailed interpretation of the **food** intake in relation to the requirements for health and wellbeing for Olivia
> - a detailed interpretation of the **fluid** intake with specific reference to the requirements for health and wellbeing for Olivia
> - a detailed interpretation of the **nutritional programme**, making specific reference to factors affecting **digestion** and **absorption** of nutrients and fluids.

Guided

To eat for health and wellbeing, in line with the Eatwell Guide, Olivia should:

- Eat the correct amount to ....

  ....

- Eat plenty of foods rich in ....

  ....

- Cut back on fat ....

  Improve ....

  The higher intake recorded on Tuesday reflects the consumption of ....

- Ensure adequate intakes of ....

  ....

  ....

  As a female endurance athlete, Olivia should ensure she has ....

- Keep within sensible limits for ....

  ....

Unit 13
Guided

- Not eat sugary foods too often ....
  ....
  ....
  ....

> The response above starts by **evaluating the food intake** in line with the Eatwell Guide for health and wellbeing. You could go on to **interpret** Olivia's **energy and nutrient requirements**, comparing her food intake to her calculated requirements and the balance of intake to her expenditure.

For a more detailed interpretation of Olivia's food intake it would be helpful to predict her energy and nutrient requirements. I have estimated energy requirements using the Harris-Benedict equation for calculating BMR and a physical activity factor of 1.725 at 2461 kcal per day.

BMR = 655.1 + (9.56 × 57) + (1.85 × 168) − (4.68 × 18)

655.1 + 544.92 + 310.8 − 84.24

1510.82 − 84.24 = <u>1426.58 kcal</u>

TER = 1426.58 × 1.725 = <u>2461 kcal</u>

Some days Olivia is close to meeting this requirement; on others she is either well below or significantly above. However, it is to be expected that her intake will vary, dependent on the exact nature of her training schedule, i.e. her energy requirements will not be exactly the same day in, day out. Her average daily energy intake is ....
....

Her lowest intake day is ....
....

Her highest intake day is ....
....

Olivia has relatively low intake on Saturday ....
....
....

> Continue with an interpretation of Olivia's carbohydrate, protein and fat requirements.
> When you **interpret** nutrition requirements, you should look to try to draw meaning, purpose or explanation.
> When you **state**, you give a definition or example, or give an answer to a calculation.

As Olivia's training level is high, she is likely to have a larger requirement for carbohydrate. She is training between 45 mins to 2 hours, five days of the week. On training days, she is likely to have a carbohydrate requirement of 6–7 g per kilogram of body weight per day: 6 × 57 = 342 g; 7 × 57 = 399 g. As a percentage of her overall energy requirement, this would represent 56–65 per cent.

342 × 4 = 1368; 1368 ÷ 2461 = 0.555; 0.555 × 100 = 56%.

399 × 4 = 1596; 1596 ÷ 2461 = 0.648; 0.648 × 100 = 65%.

Olivia's average carbohydrate intake over the seven days is 333 g with a range of intakes from 275 g to 385 g. This might mean that she is not adequately refuelling between all training sessions.

Looking at her carbohydrate intake more closely, Olivia's highest carbohydrate intake is recorded on

....

....

Lowest intake is on ....

....

On Saturday where Olivia has two sessions and a hard hills session, Oliva only achieved a

carbohydrate intake of ....

....

....

As Olivia's sport is endurance focused, her protein requirements ....

....

Her range of protein intakes is from ....

....

Olivia's fat intake ranges from ....

....

When considered as a percentage of her overall calorie intake 655/2548 this represents 26%, in

line with ....

....

It may be helpful for Olivia to replace some fat in her diet with additional ....

....

....

> Go on to **evaluate** and **interpret** Olivia's **fluid intake**.
> - Start by **calculating Olivia's fluid requirements**, taking into account environmental conditions and the specific demands of the individual training sessions.
> - Report on her **current intake** from the typical nutritional programme and whether it is consistent or not.
> - Look at where **highest** and **lowest** intakes occur and what might be **impacting** on this.
> - Comment on the **types** and **quality** of fluid consumed.

Based on using the formula 1 ml per calorie of energy requirement, Olivia's fluid requirements would

be around ....

....

Unit 13
Guided

From current nutritional intake, Olivia's fluid intake is quite inconsistent, ranging from 1100-3995 ml

....

....

....

....

Olivia is not meeting her fluid intake targets on ....

....

Considering the quality of Olivia's fluid choices, ...

....

Olivia does occasionally consume a bottle of vanilla milkshake ....

....

....

> When making specific reference to factors affecting **digestion and absorption of nutrients and fluids**, ensure you:
> - make **specific reference to factors affecting** digestion and absorption
> - consider **type**, **quantity** and **timing** of **food and fluid intake**.

Before the body can make use of the energy and nutrients that food contains it has to ....

....

....

....

....

....

....

....

....

Many factors can influence the effectiveness of fluid-replacement strategies during and after

exercise. Fluid replacement can be accelerated by ....

....

....

....

....

....

Olivia might want to consider ....

....

....

....

....

....

....

> You could **conclude** your answer by summing up **key factors** that link to proposed nutritional modifications and strategies.

After undertaking a detailed interpretation of Olivia's food and fluid intake with reference to

requirements for health and wellbeing, it is clear that she ....

....

....

> **Links** To revise calculating requirements and interpreting intake relevant to health and wellbeing, see page 176 of the Revision Guide for Recommended Daily Allowance, pages 180–187 for macronutrients, micronutrients and fibre, pages 188–189 for fluids, pages 194–197 for intake for health and wellbeing, pages 201–207 for supplements and sports foods. To revise calculating BMA and TER see page 177 and for estimating carbohydrate requirements see page 215.

Unit 13
Guided

Revision question 2

Modify the nutritional programme, based on nutritional strategies, in relation to Olivia's cross-country championship over a 6 km distance.

> Refer to the information about Olivia on pages 90–92. Use the guide below which reflects one way of structuring a response. You should:
> - **propose nutritional modifications and strategies** that demonstrate relevance to Olivia's cross-country championship over a 6 km distance
> - **support the proposed modifications with justifications** that demonstrate relevance to Olivia's cross-country championship
> - **propose modifications** of the nutritional programme, making reference to the impact of factors affecting **digestion and absorption of nutrients and fluids**.

Guided

Oliva is currently training for a cross-country event four weeks away. To optimise training and competition performance, she should consider ....

....

....

....

> Continue the response by looking at **modifications** to improve Olivia's overall food and fluid intake.
> Consider the **Eatwell Guide** and Olivia's attention to:
> - **carbohydrate intake** appropriate to support her training for the event
> - **eating patterns** around her training to ensure optimal recovery
> - **use of snacks and fluids** to support optimal recovery from her training activities.

Overall Olivia has a good and varied food intake, but she needs to ....

....

....

....

As an endurance athlete, she should aim to ....

....

....

....

Her eating may need to be fitted in ....

....

....

....

Generally, she has used her rest days ....

....

....

A high fluid intake should be encouraged ....

....

....

....

....

....

> You could continue by considering modifications with reference to **pre-training and event strategies**. Think about:
> - **pre-training and competition meals** to top up liver and glycogen stores
> - **intake levels** of carbohydrate, fat, fibre, protein and accompanying **digestion**
> - **hydration and fluid replacement strategies**, bearing in mind the recommended fluid intake and timing.

Olivia's pre-training or competition meal should aim to top up ....

....

....

....

It is important to advise her not to experiment with ....

....

....

It is noted that her race start time is ....

....

....

....

> Next you could consider modifications with reference to the **during training phase and event strategies**. You could particularly think about fluid loss and replacement, and the effect of this on performance.

As long as Olivia has prepared well for the event, ...

....

....

....

> You could continue by considering modifications with reference to **post-training and event strategies**. You could particularly think about fluid loss and replacement, and the effect of this on performance. Give some thought to:
> - the importance of **refuelling**
> - the role of **carbohydrates**
> - suggestions for size, frequency and optimum timing of **snacks**
> - post-training recovery strategy including **rehydration**, relevance of sports drinks, and monitoring replacement of fluid loss.

It is important for Olivia to refuel as soon as possible after ....

....

To refuel efficiently, ...

....

....

Olivia should then aim to eat her next meal ....

....

....

It would have been helpful to know when she consumed the particular snacks each day ....

....

....

....

She should start rehydrating immediately. ....

....

....

> Next you could comment on the relevance of **sports foods and nutritional supplements**. You could consider:
> - how much sports foods and nutritional supplements are part of the current strategy and suggest **modifications**
> - **risks** versus **benefits**
> - their role in the context of **healthy food choices** and short- and long-term **goals**
> - **side effects** and considerations in experimenting with **choices**
> - specific **recommendations** relevant to the client in different **phases**.

Some endurance athletes find sports foods such as drinks, bars and gels useful to ....

....

....

....

In considering ways to modify her strategy with sports and food supplements, Olivia does not

currently ....

....

....

....

It is important to remember that supplements should be safe, ...

....

....

Olivia might want to consider the use of beetroot juice, ...

....

....

....

Olivia may want to consider experimenting with caffeine

If Olivia is going to consider implementing caffeine or beetroot juice on race day,

> **Links** To revise modifications and recommendations, see pages 174–179 of the Revision Guide to revise nutritional principles, pages 190–193 to revise digestion, absorption and control, pages 194–198 to revise nutritional intake for health and wellbeing, pages 208–211 for nutritional strategies page 218 for modifying a nutritional programme.

Unit 13
Guided

Revision question 3

Recommend nutritional guidance for Olivia based on her phase of training.

> Refer to the information about Olivia on pages 90–92. Use the guide below, which reflects one way of structuring an answer. You should:
> - demonstrate specific **relevance** of nutritional guidance to the **phase** of Olivia's sporting event
> - make specific reference to the **impact** on Olivia of factors affecting **digestion and absorption** of nutrients and fluids based on their **phase of training**.

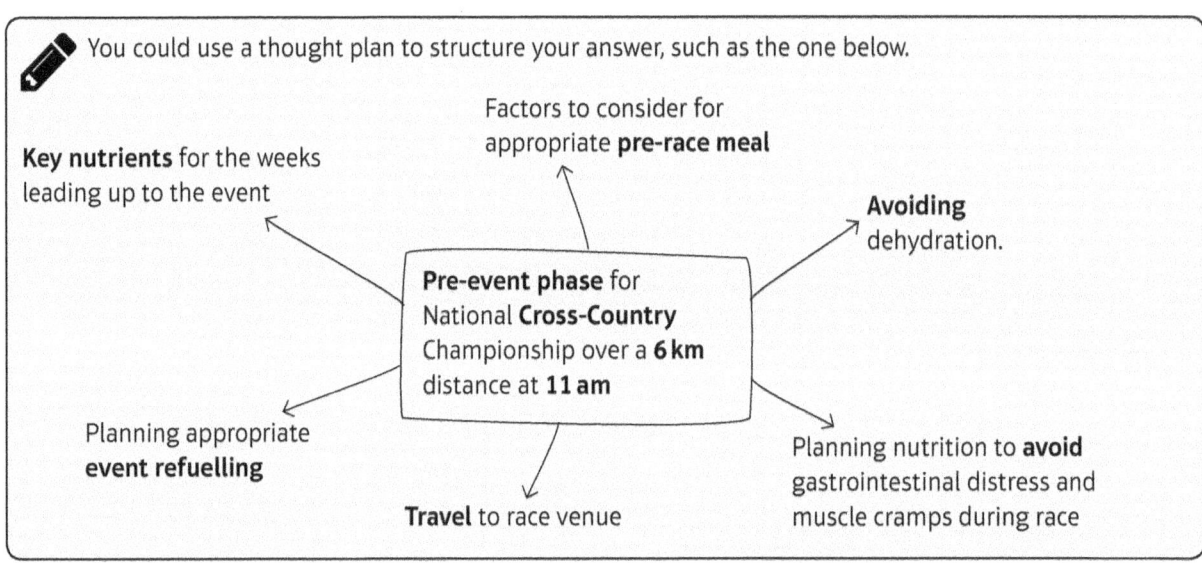

You could use a thought plan to structure your answer, such as the one below.

Guided

Endurance events challenge energy and fluid stores, so athletes should ....

....

....

Many of the principles of preparing for an event mirror those of the training diet. Nutrition demands focus on maintaining energy and fluid requirements, and competing at an optimum weight, free from injury and illness. A pre-competition meal should aim to top up ....

....

....

> The opening of the response relates to **endurance events and nutritional challenges** and the **requirements of endurance athletes in the pre-event phase of training**.
>
> You could continue by recommending a meal plan to ensure that Olivia achieves adequate fuel and fluid availability for the race at 11.00am, also considering what she eats the night before and what to do if she suffers from race-day nerves.

For a meal plan leading up to an 11am cross-country championship, I would recommend Olivia to plan her nutrition intake for the night before. If she takes a meal ....

....

....

....

If Olivia eats her meal early she should ....

....

....

On race day, Olivia should have ....

....

Looking at Olivia's typical nutritional programme, familiar examples of race-day breakfasts would

include ....

....

....

Olivia's pre-event meal should be made up of familiar foods and provide ....

....

....

....

....

If Olivia suffers from race-day nerves ....

....

Sipping on sports drinks leading up to the start will help ....

....

> You should **conclude** with the **expected outcomes** from your recommended nutritional strategies.

Developing sound nutritional strategies should ....

....

....

Meeting her energy and fluid requirements should help her ....

....

....

....

Links To revise application of relevant phase of training, see pages 208–211 and 219–220 of the Revision Guide.

END OF TASK

Answers

Unit 1: Sport and Exercise Physiology

Revision paper 1 – guided (pages 2–20)

1. (a) Individual responses. Example answer:
   Joe's training programme will recruit muscle fibres as the muscles are put under physical stress, helping the muscles to grow and adapt in size. The process of vasoconstriction and vasodilation will increase the amount of blood to the working muscles to ensure they have a constant supply of oxygen. When under stress, Joe's muscles will contract and relax against each other causing microscopic tears in the muscle fibres which his body will repair after the session, enabling them to increase in strength and in some cases also in size.

   (b) Individual responses. Example answer:
   An initial increase is seen in Joe's heart rate, called an anticipatory rise, because the brain secretes the hormones adrenaline and noradrenaline which increase the heart rate. This results in an increase in blood flow which helps supply the body with oxygen and nutrients to the muscles which are about to be worked. This process is a subconscious action which is used to physiologically prepare Joe for exercise.

   (c) Individual responses. Answers might include **two** of the following, for example.
   1. Through training, Joe's ligaments and tendons have been subjected to an array of physical stresses which cause slight damage. The body produces collagen to heal the damage caused by the stress exercise places on them. This helps to strengthen the ligaments and tendons making them more resistant to fatigue.
   2. Exercise produces tiny tears in Joe's muscle fibres. Sometimes tears in the muscle fibres cause pain and swelling in the muscle tissue. Protein is used to repair the tears in the muscle and make the muscle tissue stronger. The stronger the muscle tissues, the more they can be used before they begin to fatigue.
   3. Delayed onset of muscle soreness (DOMS) occurs between 24 and 48 hours after Joe has finished exercise. The pain he experiences is because of the structural damage to muscle cells. Over time, Joe's musculoskeletal system will become more resistant to fatigue as he becomes more used to his training regime.

   Further answers may be possible, for example referring to waste products and energy depletion.

   (d) Individual responses. Answers might include:
   Joe's fitness training programme will use all three energy systems which support the aerobic and anaerobic demands of each exercise. For Joe to be successful he needs to rely on the ATP-PC system, lactate system and aerobic energy system.

   ATP-PC energy system
   - ATP-PC is the first energy system and it provides enough power for a few seconds of all-out exercise. The energy system relies on the creatine phosphate stored in the muscles. The enzyme that controls the breakdown of PC is called creatine kinase. This system works by splitting creatine from the phosphate molecule to produce energy.
   - The ATP-PC system helps Joe with his training programme because it produces high intensity, anaerobic energy which can be used for 8–10 seconds of work.
   - The by-products produced by this system are creatine and phosphate. These molecules need energy to re-join, so cannot be used again until they have had time to replenish. There is a small amount of creatine phosphate in our body. This limits the amount of energy that can be produced using this system.

   Lactate or anaerobic glycolysis energy system
   - The second energy system that Joe will use is the lactate system. This is also known as anaerobic glycolysis. This energy system lasts for 30 seconds to a few minutes, depending on the intensity. The lactate system requires glucose to produce energy without oxygen.
   - This energy system is important because it produces high intensity energy which can be used for longer than the ATP-PC system and can replenish quickly.
   - The by-products produced by this system are lactate. These by-products will affect Joe's performance because when lactate accumulates in muscle fibres it increases the blood's' activity. If the lactate cannot be removed, the acidity prevents the energy system from working and it is at this point that blood lactate is produced faster than it can be used aerobically. Joe may experience muscle fatigue and intramuscular pain if the exercise intensity remains high. This is because the hydrogen ions in the muscle increase which inhibits sustained muscular contractions.

   Aerobic energy system
   - The final energy system to be evaluated is the aerobic system. This system lasts for hours as it relies on a constant supply of oxygen.
   - Carbon dioxide and water are by-products for this energy system which uses oxygen to break down glucose or fat.
   - The aerobic energy system works by using oxygen to break down glucose/glycogen or fat which produces energy which can be used to resynthesise ATP. By using oxygen, the glucose molecule can be totally broken down to produce 18 times more energy than it does when broken down anaerobically.
   - This energy system will affect Joe's performance by producing energy for long periods of time which will allow him to perform at a less intense level of activity.

   Continuum of energy systems
   - To summarise, energy systems are viewed as a continuum as none of the systems act independently.
   - Joe's training programme provides a balanced mix of activities which will vary in intensity throughout the session. There will be elements of anaerobic and aerobic activities during each session. This provides Joe with a complete body workout and enables efficiencies to be made in the body systems to assist him in being able to meet the demands placed upon the body, without experiencing extreme fatigue.

2. (a) Individual responses. Example answer:
   Arteriovenous oxygen difference (a-VO$_2$ diff) is the difference in the amount of oxygen found between arterial and venous blood.
   The difference between stage 1 and stage 2 will increase the a-VO$_2$ diff as the intensity of exercise increases between swimming and cycling due to the amount of force placed on the body. At stage 1, the 2.4-mile swim presents challenges with resistance from the current in the open water. However, the duration of cycling at stage 2 is significantly longer at 112 miles and the hilly and windy conditions will present challenges.
   The difference between arterial and venous blood increases due to the working muscles needing more oxygen from the arterial blood because this vessel carries blood under a higher pressure. Therefore, the oxygen content of the venous return decreases because more oxygen is absorbed.

(b) Individual responses. Example answer:
Due to the duration of Gabriella's event taking place over a 24-hour period, there will be limited opportunities to take a substantial amount of food on board. Therefore, Gabriella will need energy replacement substances such as protein shakes and carbohydrate gels. Protein is needed to help repair the muscle damage caused by prolonged physical activity. Gabriella will also need a supply of carbohydrates to help provide the body with energy to assist her in completing each stage of the event.

(c) Individual responses. Example answer:
Neuromuscular fatigue is common after exposure to prolonged exercise. The motor units from the central nervous system become compromised, preventing the units from being able to conduct their normal functions effectively. The loss of motor unit performance will have a detrimental effect on Gabriella, causing a decrease in performance. Acetylcholine is released by the parasympathetic nervous system to stimulate skeletal muscles. However, when this gets depleted the muscle fibres are unable to sustain repeated muscle contractions.

(d) Individual responses. Answers might include:
- The predicted outside temperature for Gabriella's competition is high. As Gabriella exercises, she will also be generating heat as a waste product of exercise. To help combat the excess heat, Gabriella's body will work hard to cool it down even when working at extreme temperatures. To do this, the body will produce sweat using an array of heat loss techniques.
- Heat will be lost through the evaporation of sweat during the cycling and running stages. Heat loss through convection will occur during the first stage as Gabriella will lose the excess heat that has been generated through heating the water which surrounds Gabriella's body. Gabriella will also lose heat through the process of conduction as the air flow around Gabriella will assist in cooling her down as she competes in stages 2 and 3.
- When Gabriella sweats, she will lose electrolytes and water during the cooling process. The more Gabriella sweats, the greater the depletion of electrolytes. It is important that these are replaced through fluid intake to assist in diminishing the symptoms of fatigue that will be experienced as part of a 24-hour race. This will also ensure the nervous system continues to function. If this does not occur throughout the competition, it is likely that Gabriella will become very ill.
- The temperature that is predicted for Gabriella's race is considered to be an extreme temperature. Exposure to extreme heat temperatures will produce an earlier onset of sweating, if heat acclimatisation does not occur. This is because Gabriella's body will be trying to combat the excess external and internal heat.
- Based on the predicted temperatures, it is clear that Gabriella will suffer from excessive water loss over the 24-hour duration. It is important that Gabriella ensures that her water loss does not exceed the amount of fluid consumed or this will result in a negative fluid balance.
- Dehydration can cause a decrease in blood plasma which over time can result in an inadequate level of blood volume.

3 (a) Individual responses. Example answer:
1 Type I muscle fibres will be used when Parvez is working at a low intensity for a long duration, e.g. jogging.
2 Type IIa muscle fibres will be used to provide high intensity energy for moderate periods, e.g. when Parvez completes a set of bench presses.
Type IIx muscle fibres will be used to provide high intensity energy for short periods of time, e.g. Parvez will use this type when he performs a 1RM back squat.

(b) Individual responses. Answers might include:
The onset of blood lactate (OBLA) occurs when the level of lactate in the blood reaches 4 mmol/L and above. 4 mmol/L is known as the lactate threshold.
OBLA happens when the amount of lactate produced exceeds more than what can be used aerobically through the energy system continuum.
When exercise continues when blood lactate is above 4 mmol/L, there is an increase in the number of hydrogen ions in muscle tissue and this causes intramuscular pain and fatigue.
With HIIT training, Parvez will experience OBLA due to the intense nature of his training programme leading to anaerobic respiration occurring during the exercise bout. The rest period between the work periods helps to reduce the level of blood lactate using EPOC.

(c) Individual responses. Example answer:
Energy sources can become depleted in the training sessions and within the recovery period. This is why it is important for Parvez to have sufficient rest in between training to ensure the muscles and energy systems have enough time to recover. Parvez will experience delayed onset of muscle soreness (DOMS). This is a discomfort which is commonly experienced within the muscles between 24–48 hours after exercising. DOMS occurs as a direct result of HIIT. The pain and stiffness experienced as a result of DOMS can inhibit the muscles' potential. This is the same for the VO_2 max result as the test relies on the leg muscles to sustain muscle contractions for a long period which supports the view that it was fatigue that has led to poor improvements between week 4 and week 8.

(d) Individual responses. Answers might include:
- Over the 12-week training period, Parvez has improved his VO_2 max result at each stage. However, between weeks 4 and 8 the change in test results was small.
- An increase in Parvez's VO_2 max shows that there is a higher rate of oxygen absorption and usage. This gives the potential for Parvez to train at higher intensities before muscle tissue demand for oxygen uptake exceeds supply.
- The higher the VO_2 max, the more efficient the cardiovascular system will be.
- A greater VO_2 max allows Parvez to continue his exercise programme and its subsequent activities for longer, delaying the onset of fatigue.
- An increase in Parvez's VO_2 max also assists him to make a faster post-exercise recovery as his body can return to its resting state quicker.
- Parvez will be able to withstand a higher amount of lactate in the blood due to the body becoming more efficient at using oxygen to supply the working muscles.
- The change in frequency of the training programme, back to three times a week has enabled Parvez to continue to make progress in improving his cardiovascular fitness. The change in frequency has also reduced the effect of DOMS as Parvez is able to use the cardiovascular system more effectively to reduce the number of hydrogen ions found in the muscle tissue following anaerobic activity.
- EPOC becomes more effective at minimising the effect of fatigue on the muscles and cardiovascular system.
- Parvez's results in week 12 have improved since the training sessions were reduced to three per week as opposed to every other day between weeks 5 and 8. By reducing the frequency, there has been an increase in VO_2 max results which now puts Parvez in the average category rather than the poor category he first started with.
- Providing Parvez has a sufficient amount of rest in between training sessions, his muscle system will be able to adapt to the HIIT exercises. This allows the muscles to increase in size (hypertrophy).

- As a result of hypertrophy, Parvez's muscles will be able to generate more force so that they can overcome a greater amount of resistance. This is because there is an increase in the number of muscle fibres that can be recruited to contract.
- Over time, Parvez's muscles will adapt to HIIT. HIIT uses heavy loads, i.e. body weight exercises. This causes Type IIa muscle fibres to adapt to the anaerobic nature of the training programme. These muscle fibres behave more like Type IIx, enabling them to produce greater force at a higher intensity. This enables Parvez to complete more repetitions and withstand a greater amount of force being placed on the muscle.

4 (a) Individual responses. Answers might include:
1 Vasoconstriction – occurs in blood vessels that do not need an enhanced blood supply during exercise, while vasodilation occurs in active muscles by increasing the dilation of arterioles, increasing the amount of blood flow to the muscles.
2 Increased cardiac output – occurs as the volume of blood pumped out of the heart per minute increases when compared to resting levels, which enables Naseem to supply her working muscles with a sufficient supply of oxygen to sustain repeated muscle contractions.
3 Stroke volume increases – when exercising due to the increased demand placed on the cardiovascular system.

(b) Individual responses. Example answer:
1 During the first few minutes of Naseem's training session, in the pool or on land, her body will be fuelled by anaerobic metabolism due to oxygen needed to be present for aerobic metabolism. Naseem's aerobic energy system will become more efficient as it will have a greater capacity to generate energy aerobically the more often she trains.
2 Naseem's training programme, in the pool or on land, will be fuelled by carbohydrate and fat stores which are used through anaerobic glycolysis. The intensity and duration of Naseem's training sessions will determine the fuel source used. Naseem's training programme, in the pool or on land, will mostly use carbohydrates as the fuel source because she will be training about at 80 per cent of her VO_2 max.

(c) Individual responses. Example answer:
Naseem will use her glycogen stores in the muscles to break down the glycogen enzymes into glucose which is used in aerobic metabolism. By Naseem having a high carbohydrate diet, this will increase the stores of carbohydrates in the muscles.
An increased level of carbohydrates in Naseem's muscles will provide her with the energy she needs to be able to compete in her time trial.
By having more carbohydrates in the body, she will be able to have an immediate energy source which will assist her in swimming faster.

(d) Individual responses. Answers might include:
- Naseem's training programme has been effective at putting the cardiovascular and respiratory systems under an increased pressure causing them to adapt to the elevated training loads. This is supported by the results in Table 4 in which all results have shown a significant improvement in Naseem's fitness.
- Through sustained aerobic training, Naseem will have increased her stroke volume which slows down her cardiac cycle because the heart has become more efficient in supplying the working muscles with oxygenated blood. This adaptation can be evidenced in the decrease in Naseem's resting heart rate.
- Naseem's maximal cardiac output will assist in supplying the working muscles with oxygen in a more efficient way. An increased maximal output will also help Naseem to reduce her recovery time following her race.
- Table 4 shows that there has been a significant improvement in her lung function volumes. This will assist Naseem to breathe in more oxygen per breath, ensuring that the body has enough oxygen to maintain aerobic functioning.
- The cardiovascular system becomes more efficient as the respiratory muscles increase in strength which enables the intercostal muscles to relax and contract, forcing more air into the lungs in each breath.
- The higher the contraction rate, the greater the volume of air. This effect is evidenced by the 700 ml increase in the forced vital capacity following the test results of the peak flow measure.
- Naseem's tidal volume, vital capacity and residual volume increase with sustained aerobic training. Naseem will be able to utilise the increased amount of oxygen present in the system and will delay her reaching lactate threshold through her 200 m butterfly race. This will mean that she will be able to compete at a faster pace.
- The delay in the onset of blood lactate is a result of Naseem's increased VO_2 max because Naseem is able to utilise the maximal amount of oxygen per minute which will assist her in swimming a fast time for her race.
- Naseem's body will adapt and her respiratory rate will increase to aid the delivery of more oxygen to the working muscles. However, as Naseem's body adapts to the training regime her respiratory rate will decrease as her respiratory system becomes more efficient at supplying the cardiovascular system with oxygen. Therefore, Naseem will be able to perform for longer at a higher intensity.

Revision paper 2 (pages 21–36)

1 (a) Individual responses. Example answer:
Synovial fluid production increases with a thorough warm-up, which helps ease movement and increases the range of movement. The synovial fluid also reduces viscosity, which helps reduce friction. Joints are protected by cartilage on the ends of long bones to act as shock absorption and the synovial fluid nourishes and lubricates the articular cartilage so that the tissue stays healthy and uninjured.

(b) Individual responses. Example answer:
Muscle fibre types and motor units are recruited relative to the exercise demand and frequency of stimulation. The recruitment of motor units, which cause muscle fibres to contract, work on an all or nothing principle. The stimulus from the motor neuron to the muscle fibre needs to be strong enough for the muscle fibre to contract, or no contraction will be produced. At high intensity, Leah's motor neurons will send strong signals to ensure that all muscle fibres contract.

(c) Individual responses. Example answer:
1 Muscle spindles sense changes in muscle length. They signal the muscle to regulate contraction to avoid overstretching. Muscle spindles increase motor unit recruitment and increase strength of contraction to decrease rate muscle being stretched (as in deceleration).
2 Golgi tendon organs sense changes in muscle tension. They signal motor neurons to relax, causing the muscle to relax to avoid overstretching (myotatic reflex). They also regulate tension in muscles, causing relaxation before the tension in the tendon becomes too great and causes tissue destruction.

(d) Individual responses. Example answers:
Catecholamines:
- Adrenaline (80 per cent) and noradrenaline (20 per cent) secretion increases in response to exercise.

Cardiovascular system:
- Acts to increase heart rate – stimulating cardiac output; increased blood flow; increased potential oxygen for energy production and removal of carbon dioxide; enhances performance as more energy available.

- Increased peripheral resistance of blood vessels – smooth muscle in arterial walls stimulated to contract; increase in blood pressure and enhanced delivery of oxygen, which enhances performance through more oxygen to contribute to energy production.
- This all contributes to decreased blood flow to the digestive and urinary systems as the blood flow to muscles increases to aid performance.

Respiratory system:
- Dilation of bronchioles – relaxation of smooth muscle in walls aids increased breathing rate and potential increased oxygen intake and removal of carbon dioxide. Helps energy production to fuel exercise.

Energy systems:
- Cortisol secretion increases in response to exercise. Main role is to raise blood sugar – stimulates liver to convert fatty acids into glucose as exercise duration increases – continued fuel for performance.
- Increased breakdown of glycogen into glucose, for circulation in blood and energy production – continued performance.
- The more glycogen is used, the more is released from liver into muscles. This will provide further energy for exercise particularly if the competition event goes on for more than 30 minutes.
- Human growth hormone (HGH) secretion increases in response to exercise. This stimulates the release of fatty acids in response to increased stress on skeletal muscles (due to the demands of exercise). Large muscle groups are used when competing in CrossFit. As the exercise intensity (resistance) increases and the rest intervals decrease, HGH release is simulated. The release of HGH provides additional energy for prolonged performance, ultimately delaying the effects of fatigue for the athlete.

Muscular system:
- Testosterone (not so prevalent in women) increases in response to training such as CrossFit where there is a high volume of exercise at high intensity, with little rest period. It helps to prevent catabolism of muscle tissue and increase anabolism of muscle tissue, working to improve muscle strength and performance.
- Helps with growth of tissue in recovery, which in turn will increase muscle strength and aid performance.

2 (a) Individual responses. Example answer:
Fatigue is caused by depletion of energy stores (CP, glucose and glycogen stores) and an accumulation of waste products – lactic acid, carbon dioxide and neuromuscular fatigue which reduces CNS signalling or muscle function.

The effects on performance of depleted energy stores means that there is less energy available, so the rate of ATP production and resynthesis decreases. The muscle force and power production is limited, which will reduce performance. Neuromuscular fatigue will lead to an increase in hydrogen accumulation, a lower pH, and a decrease in calcium release for muscle contraction.

(b) Individual responses. Example answer:
Excess post-exercise oxygen consumption (EPOC) occurs post-exercise where heavy breathing will help to elevate oxygen levels. The additional oxygen will help to break down lactic acid, which will help to replenish the ATP. Oxygen helps to resynthesise and replenish ATP and PC, with 50 per cent replenished within 20–48 seconds and 99 per cent replenished within 2–4 minutes. Resaturation of myoglobin is usually completed within 2–4 minutes and allows for oxygen to be transported to the mitochondria for energy breakdown. Lactic acid is 70 per cent removed with EPOC via the aerobic energy system. To replace glycogen stores, this may take 24–48 hours. As Jamie's event is very intense, his glycogen stores may not fully recover between the rounds.

(c) Individual responses. Example answer:
Jamie needs to replace the fluid and electrolytes he has lost. He should be consuming around 1.5 times the amount of fluid lost within the 2 hours following his race. He should use isotonic or hypotonic drinks, which will help him to replace the fluids and electrolytes he has lost faster than water alone. Jamie needs to eat/drink carbohydrate-rich sources to resynthesise muscle glycogen and replenish his carbohydrate stores. He also needs to take in protein to help protein synthesis to help repair the micro damage to his muscles.

(d) Individual responses. Answers might include:
- Jamie is overtraining and this is affecting his performance levels.
- There is an imbalance in Jamie's training programme as in addition to the training load increasing, the volume of training is also increasing and the recovery time decreasing.
- There appears to be an inadequate recovery time relative to the volume of training and the intensity of training, so this will increase Jamie's level of fatigue. His subsequent performance within training and competition will decrease as he is not fully recovered.
- The training load has increased, as identified by the increased intensity within the training sessions, although not by much over 12 weeks. When coupled with the increase in training volume from the number of training sessions within the week, which has doubled his training volume from week 1, with no additional rest period, this will lead to incomplete recovery and decreased performance.
- Inadequate sleep and rest will eventually lead to decreased immune function and Jamie will end up getting more colds, which will affect his training and performance.
- His muscle tissue will also be insufficiently repaired before his next bout of training which, over time, can lead to overuse injuries and inflammation. Jamie will have an increased susceptibility to muscle soreness and overuse injuries, due to the incomplete recovery of his muscle tissue, and will suffer decreased performance.
- Jamie's endocrine system may also become imbalanced in response to overtraining.
- Cortisol production will increase, which may lead to a decreased immune response and leave Jamie more susceptible to infection. If, when measured, the levels do not return to normal within 24 hours, this can indicate overtraining.
- Growth hormone will increase secretion in response to the increased cortisol levels, which helps aid repair and recovery, though will also increase lactate production. This may contribute to Jamie's muscle soreness.
- Both adrenaline and noradrenaline increase in the early stages of overtraining, though there is a decreased sensitivity to their effects, which may dull Jamie's responsiveness and reaction time at the start of a race and decrease his performance. Resting levels decrease which can lead to an increased amount of time for the heart rate to return to normal following exercise, increasing Jamie's fatigue.
- In the later stages, sympathetic nervous system activity decreases and there is less release of adrenaline and noradrenaline, which also increases fatigue.
- The increased SNS activity and adrenaline and noradrenaline release can lead to poor sleep patterns and insufficient rest and recovery, thus affecting his performance levels.

3 (a) Individual responses. Example answer:
1 The diaphragm and intercostal muscles are strengthened as Devon will breathe more deeply during exercise. This allows for greater expansion of the chest.

2   During exercise Devon's tidal volume increases as the breaths she takes become deeper and the accessory muscles support forcible exhalation during exercise, aiding oxygen delivery and carbon dioxide removal.

3   Respiratory rate increases as the number of breaths Devon takes per minute increases. This helps supply sufficient oxygen to meet the increased demand. Along with increased tidal volume, this increases minute ventilation – the volume of air breathed in per minute.

(b) Individual responses. Example answer:
Regular aerobic training increases cardiac muscle hypertrophy of the left ventricle. This increases the strength of the contraction and more blood can be forced out of the heart under greater pressure, so it reaches its destination quicker. During exercise, more blood enters the heart. This increases the pressure within the ventricles and stretches the cardiac muscle. The increased pressure in the heart causes the contractions to become more forceful which increases the amount of blood pumped out of the left ventricle per beat (stroke volume). This allows oxygen transport and venous return to increase. As the stroke volume and blood pressure increase, so too does the cardiac output, the volume of blood pumped from the heart in 1 minute, which increases blood circulation and the efficiency of the cardiovascular system. In response to training, ventricular filling increases which increases the diastole phase of the cardiac cycle and allows for filling of the ventricle. This also increases the stretch on the ventricle and increases the stroke volume.

(c) Individual responses. Example answer:
Human growth hormone (HGH) release will increase during and following heavy resistance exercise training. HGH aids muscle hypertrophy and repair of muscle tissue which leads to increased strength and power. Adrenaline and noradrenaline secretion will increase, causing an increase in heart rate and blood flow. This increases oxygen and glucose supply to the muscles. Long-term resistance training increases resting cortisol levels which can increase anti-inflammatory effects and help with tissue repair. This will aid recovery from training and help Devon to increase hypertrophy and subsequently strength and power.

(d) Individual responses. Example answers:
Measurement of VO$_2$max
- The maximal amount of oxygen you can consume and utilise in 1 minute, relative to your bodyweight. It is usually determined by a treadmill test, where the participant breathes into a Douglas bag, which is then examined using a gas analyser. It is reached when oxygen consumption plateaus for 30 seconds to 1 minute.

Influence of VO$_2$max on performance
- To improve her VO$_2$ max, Devon would need to be working at 60 per cent maximum heart rate (MHR) minimum.
- By increasing her VO$_2$ max, her respiratory and cardiovascular systems will have become more efficient at taking in and utilising the oxygen, which will help provide an increased oxygen supply for energy production via the aerobic energy system and prolong her performance.

Measurement of anaerobic threshold
- Usually measured with a graded exercise test, and velocity increased at regular intervals, with blood lactate tested at each interval.
- Each blood lactate measure is plotted against time. Where there is a sharp increase in the level of lactate measured, this is the anaerobic threshold.

Influence of anaerobic threshold on performance
- Anaerobic threshold is approximately 80 per cent MHR, which is the level where anaerobic fitness can be improved. Devon would need to be regularly training at this level in order to improve her anaerobic threshold.
- If Devon's anaerobic threshold is higher, then she will reach her anaerobic threshold after a longer time than if she were untrained. This means that the capacity of the anaerobic system to produce energy is increased and it will take longer for the onset of anaerobic threshold to occur, which will benefit her performance in the row.
- To improve her anaerobic threshold, she could use interval training with longer work and shorter rest periods.

Measurement of anaerobic power
- The Wingate test is usually used to determine anaerobic power and involves using a cycle ergometer and pedalling against a set resistance for a set time. This will determine the maximal power developed in a short time and reflects the energy output of the ATP-PC and lactate energy systems.

Influence of anaerobic power on performance
- As anaerobic power contributes to short bursts within a performance, this will benefit Devon's row, not only with each stroke, but if she needed a burst of speed towards the end of the race.
- She could use the Wingate test as part of her training, and could include plyometric exercises and hill sprints to help boost this.

4 (a) Individual responses. Example answer:
1   Hypoxia – occurs when the body has insufficient access to oxygen. At altitude, the air is oxygen-deficient, so the lower carbon dioxide levels cause the brain's blood vessels to contract.
2   Heart rate – will increase, due to the decreased oxygen availability in the air at altitude, in an attempt to meet the demands for oxygen during Asanti's training sessions.
3   Asanti may experience tachycardia – where his resting heart rate is higher than normal and more than 100 beats per minute.

(b) Individual responses. Example answer:
The hypothalamus acts as the body's thermostat for temperature regulation of around 37°C. It ensures homeostasis so that bodily functions and core temperature are maintained by initiating responses due to heat gain or heat loss. Convection happens in air by carrying away air heated by the body into the surroundings. In water, convection happens via the water around the body; heat from the body warms water surrounding it, the heat is then carried away from the body by the water flowing over the skin.
The quicker the air or water moves around the body, the greater the amount of heat lost from the body. Conduction involves the transfer of heat via warming any cooler surfaces in contact with the skin and the rate of heat loss depends on the temperature difference between the skin and surroundings. Evaporation is the body's main mechanism to prevent overheating. Breathing or sweating transfers heat from the body to the environment through water vaporisation. When the sweat reaches the skin surface, it cools and evaporates.

(c) Individual responses. Example answer:
Lack of oxygen stimulates the release of erythropoietin, which is responsible for red blood cell production. Altitude training decreases blood plasma volume, though this will begin to increase slightly as Asanti acclimatises to the altitude. The haemoglobin concentration within the blood will increase in response to altitude acclimatisation, which enables the transportation of larger quantities of oxygen around the body. Increased capillarisation will allow for increased oxygen delivery to the muscles. Due to the enhanced capillarisation from training at altitude, myoglobin stores increase. This ensures a better supply of oxygen for energy production to prolong exercise and performance. The mitochondrial density within Asanti's

muscles would increase, allowing for increased use of fat for energy and as fuel for exercise, giving him the ability to continue his endurance performance for longer.

(d) Individual responses. Example answers:

Effects of adaptation to excessive heat
- The six weeks of training to be able to perform better in excessive heat conditions, above sea level, will cause adaptations in the athlete's response to performing in heat.
- This will benefit his performance when returning to the usual environment, where he will perform at a higher level for longer as the negative impact of excessive heat on performance will be delayed.

Adaptations to excessive heat will include:

Increased sweat production
- In response to high temperatures sweating increases. It involves the secretion of sweat on to the surface of the skin and acts to cool the body.
- If the sweat remains on the skin, it provides an effective cooling process through evaporation. This helps to regulate body temperature in the heat.

Reduced electrolyte concentration in sweat
- There is less sodium content within the sweat, which helps with retaining water in the body and maintaining fluid levels to prevent dehydration.

Increased blood plasma volume
- Increased temperatures stimulate the body into producing more blood plasma. This can aid performance and lead to increased VO_2 max and cardiac output as the blood is less viscous and flows more easily.

Earlier onset of sweating
- The result of sweating earlier means that the body can cool the skin and core temperatures sooner and maintain homeostasis. This will ensure that fatigue due to the heat and hyperthermia does not occur and the perceived exertion will be lower.

Effects on aerobic performance
- Submaximal aerobic performance is limited more by central fatigue in hot conditions, which will impair Asanti's ability to sustain muscle contraction in prolonged activity.

Effects on anaerobic performance
- In a hot environment, maximal anaerobic activity is limited by oxygen delivery to active muscle via the cardiovascular system, while maintaining thermoregulatory homeostasis.

Impact of heat on anaerobic and aerobic performance
- Playing football in a hot environment will initially cause a decrease in Asanti's performance within high intensity anaerobic activity – in this situation, an increased heart rate may not occur. His core body temperature will be increased due to the environmental conditions and the heat produced through muscle activity.
- As football contains both anaerobic and aerobic components, it is logical that factors affecting both submaximal and maximal fatigue will influence performance.

Unit 2: Functional Anatomy

Revision paper 1 – guided (pages 38–49)

1   Example answer:
    The bundle of His is located in the heart and its function is to send electrical impulses that regulate the heartbeat.

2   Example answer:
    Lateral: away from the midline of the body
    Peripheral: away from the centre of the body

3   Example answer:
    The alveoli are small air sacs found in the lungs and allow the transfer of oxygen breathed in through the lungs to the capillaries. Carbon dioxide also diffuses across their surface to leave the body via the lungs.

4   Individual response for **one** of the following. Example answers:

    Removal of waste products
    The cardiovascular system is responsible for delivering oxygen and nutrients around the body especially during exercise when there is higher demand. During exercise, waste products such as carbon dioxide and lactate are produced. The cardiovascular system must remove these to ensure the body can keep exercising.

    Control of blood flow
    The cardiovascular system is responsible for delivering oxygen and nutrients around the body especially during exercise when there is higher demand. During exercise, the cardiovascular system controls blood flow. This ensures the blood is shunted towards the working muscles and away from areas that don't need it, providing vital nutrients and oxygen to allow the muscles to exercise for longer.

5   Example answer:
    The cardiac cycle is the blood flow through the heart to create a heartbeat. Diastole is when the atria contract to send the blood down to the ventricles. When the ventricle is full, the valves close to block a backflow of blood into the atria. Systole is the ventricular contraction phase of the cardiac cycle. When the ventricles are full following diastole, they contract to send blood either to the lungs for re-oxygenation or to the body so the muscles can use the oxygen-rich blood.

6   Example answer:
    When an athlete wants to exercise, a message is received from the brain which then transmits to the muscles the athlete wants to use. To do this, there are nerve impulses which are an electrical current that run from the CNS (central nervous system) to the muscles. The neuromuscular junction is the place where the nerve and muscle meet. The gap between the nerve and the muscle is called the synaptic cleft. When the nerve transmits its signal, the pre-synaptic membrane releases acetylcholine which is a neurotransmitter. This diffuses across the gap between the nerve and muscle and creates an electrical signal. If this signal is big enough, the muscle will contract to produce movement.

7   Example answer:
    Carbon dioxide is a waste product created in the process of respiration and needs to be removed from the body. During exercise, the body produces more carbon dioxide and it needs to be exhaled to prevent lactate building up in the blood. During exercise, the body/muscles need more energy, so more oxygen is used which produces more carbon dioxide as a waste product of respiration.

8   Example answer:
    Muscles contract depending on the particular needs of the exercise. Most exercises in CrossFit require isotonic contractions as the length of the muscle changes throughout the exercise. Concentric contractions involve the shortening of the muscle to produce a contraction, for example the bicep in the upward phase of a bicep curl. Eccentric contractions are where the muscle lengthens to contract, for example the triceps in the downward phase of a bicep curl. Isometric contractions involve the muscle staying the same length while contracting, for example when exercise uses body weight only, such as the plank.

9   There are four key points you need to describe:
    1) muscles work in pairs
    2) role of agonist is to be the prime mover to produce movement
    3) role of the antagonist is to support the movement of the agonist in a muscle pair
    4) synergists are muscles that help to produce a contraction and fixators are muscles that support the movement by stabilising the joint at which the contraction is taking place.

10 Example answer:
The bones and joints in the skeleton, as well as the muscles, will need to work together to produce the required movement for the high jump as highlighted in Figure 1.
The knee
- In the knee, during take-off, the articulating bones are the tibia and femur.
- The movement at the hinge joint is extension.
- The agonist muscle working to produce this movement is the quadriceps group.
- The type of contraction in the agonist is concentric.

The vertebral column
- In the take-off phase, the vertebrae will be the bones involved in producing the movement.
- The movements at the cartilaginous joints in the vertebrae are extension and hyper extension.
- The agonists creating this movement are the erector spinae group.
- The type of contraction in the agonists is concentric.
- The muscles and bones must work together so the athlete jumps over the bar without touching it.

11 Answers should include the following points:
Fara's striking leg is in the preparation phase of the movement.
Trunk
- Type of joint – gliding
- Movement at the joint – extension
- Bones – vertebral column
- Plane of movement – sagittal

Ankle
- Type of joint – hinge
- Movement at the joint – plantarflexion
- Bones – tarsals
- Plane of movement – sagittal

Knee
- Type of joint – hinge
- Movement at the joint – extension
- Bones – femur, fibula and tibia
- Plane of movement – sagittal

The three joints all need to work effectively to ensure Fara can strike the ball with maximum power and accuracy to score the penalty.

12 Answers should include the following points:
To produce the movement at position B in the picture, the hip, knee and ankle must move at the same time to ensure the technique is correct.

Knee
- The type of joint at the knee is a hinge joint which allows the knee to flex as shown in position B. The lower the squat, the harder the muscles will have to contract. They will need a more forceful contraction with more muscle fibres contracting to hold the body weight.
- The bones that articulate at the knee joint are the femur and the tibia. These act as levers to create the movement of the squat.
- The movement at position B is flexion in the knee. When the athlete moves back to position A, the knee will be extended.
- The agonist muscles creating this movement are the quadriceps muscles.
- The plane of movement that the athlete will move through during the squat is the sagittal plane on a transverse axis.
- The agonist muscles will be working eccentrically at position B as they are lengthened at this stage of the movement.

Ankle
- The type of joint at the ankle is a hinge joint which produces plantar flexion and dorsiflexion. As shown at position B, the angle at the ankle is reducing as it produces dorsiflexion movement.
- The bones that articulate at the ankle joint are the tarsals and the fibula. They allow the knee to come forward as the squat is performed.
- The movement shown from position A to position B is dorsiflexion in the ankle. When the athlete moves back to position A, the ankle will be plantarflexion.
- The agonist muscle creating this movement is the tibialis anterior; the antagonist muscles are the gastrocnemius and soleus.
- The plane of movement that the athlete will move through during the squat is the sagittal plane.
- The tibialis anterior muscles, will be working concentrically at position B as they are decreasing the angle at their ankle joint and performing dorsiflexion at this stage of the movement.

Hip
The type of joint at the hip is a ball and socket which flexes as shown at position B.
- The bones that articulate at the hip joint are the femur and the pelvis. They are long bones which allow the knee to come forward to produce the squat movement.
- The movement produced at the hip from position A to position B is flexion.
- The agonist muscle creating this movement is the rectus femoris; the antagonist muscle is the gluteus maximus.
- The plane of movement that the athlete will move through during the squat is the sagittal plane.
- The rectus femoris muscles will be contracting concentrically at position B, enabling the squat movement to happen by allowing flexion at the hip.

Revision paper 2 (pages 50–61)

1 1 Tricuspid valve
   2 Bicuspid valve
2 Example answer:
   a) Red blood cells take on and transport oxygen to the cells.
   b) Platelets stop blood loss through clotting.
3 Answers should contain **two** linked points which, in combination, provide a description of the function of arteries; for example **two** of the following points.
   - Arteries carry blood away from the heart.
   - In the main, they carry oxygenated blood.
   - Arteries split into smaller arterioles to transport oxygenated blood around the body.
4 Individual responses. Example answers:
   Chemoreceptors detect change in levels of carbon dioxide and changes in pH levels. Chemoreceptors send messages to the medulla oblongata.
   The medulla oblongata initiates an increase in breathing rate. Breathing rate can increase from 14 breaths per minute at rest to 32 breaths per minute during strenuous exercise.
5 Individual responses. Answers should contain **three** linked points which, in combination, provide a logical description of the process of bone growth, for example:
   - ossification: creating bone from cartilage
   - osteoclasts: destroying or cleaning away old bone
   - osteoblasts: cells that rebuild bone.
6 Example answer:
   Inspiration is the process of the air rushing in and lung volume increasing. During inspiration, the ribs and sternum move upwards and outwards. Expiration is the process of air being forced out and the lung volume reducing. During expiration, the ribs and sternum move downwards and inwards. During inspiration, the diaphragm contracts (flattens) while during expiration, the diaphragm relaxes (domes upwards into the chest cavity).
7 Example answer:
   Gaseous exchange is the process of oxygen moving from the lungs into the bloodstream. Before training/exercising, there is 21 per cent O_2 in the air and 0.049 per cent CO_2. When the footballer is at rest, he exhales 17 per cent O_2 and 3 per cent CO_2. When the footballer trains/exercises, he uses more oxygen and produces more CO_2, and he exhales 15 per cent O_2 and

6 per cent CO_2. This is because to maintain exercise his muscles need oxygen to produce energy and more carbon dioxide, a waste product, is produced.

8 Individual responses. Example answers:
Fibrous or fixed joints allow no movement, for example the joints found between the plates in the skull. This type of joint provides protection, e.g. the cranium protects a rugby player's brain during a scrum. Cartilaginous or slightly moveable joints allow a small amount of movement, for example the joints in between the vertebrae allow small movements which provide a rugby player with larger movements overall. Synovial or moveable joints allow a wide range of movement for rugby players, for example the hip joint and other synovial joints that are ball and socket, gliding, hinge, saddle, pivot and condyloid.

9 Individual responses. Example answers:
Ligaments attach bone to bone. Ligaments are tough fibres which limit the range of movement of a joint and provide stability. They allow flexion and extension at the knee. In the knee, the lateral and medial collateral ligaments prevent any sideways movement and the cruciate ligament prevents unwanted forward and backward movements.

10 Individual responses. Points to be made include the following when assessing the action of the back leg of the sprinter:
- Joint type: ankle/hinge
- Joint type: knee/hinge
- Movement produced at ankle: plantarflexion
- Movement produced at knee: extension
- Agonist muscle at ankle: gastrocnemius
- Agonist muscle at knee: quadriceps group
- Antagonist muscle at ankle: tibialis anterior
- Antagonist muscle at knee: hamstring group
- Type of muscular contraction at ankle: concentric/isotonic
- Type of muscular contraction at knee: concentric/isotonic

11 Individual responses. Points to be made for the extent to which the sliding filament theory describes the movement in the squat includes the following:

Initiating contraction
- Before starting the squat, the athlete must initiate contraction.
- In order for the muscle to contract isotonically, the muscle must receive an instruction to do so.
- In order for the instruction to be carried out, there needs to be sufficient stimulation from the nervous system.
- The nervous system sends impulses to generate an action potential.
- With sufficient stimulation, the neurotransmitter acetylcholine is released causing the release of calcium.

Contraction
- The nervous stimulation of the muscle causes the structures in the muscle to move.
- A myofibril is made up of sarcomeres. The sarcomere is the smallest unit in the muscle that can contract.
- As each sarcomere contracts, the length of the myofibril reduces, bunching the muscle.
- This is possible because the H zone in the sarcomere reduces or disappears, depending on the required force of contraction.
- In the presence of high levels of calcium, myosin is able to attach to the actin protein filament in the sarcomere.
- The myosin forms a cross bridge and, provided there is sufficient energy available, the myosin will be able to pull on the actin filament, shortening the muscle.
- Energy is provided by the breakdown of adenosine triphosphate (ATP) by the class of enzymes ATPase.

End of contraction
- And the muscle would relax.

12 Answers should include the following points:

Arm action in overarm throw
- To produce the movements at stages A, B and C, the elbow, shoulder and wrist joints must work together to allow the basketball player to throw the ball with the correct technique.

The elbow joint
- The bones that articulate at the elbow joint are the humerus, radius and ulna. They act as levers to produce the movement when throwing the ball forward during a chest pass.
- Movement produced at the elbow joint is extension as the movement progresses and the ball is thrown forwards, overhead through stages A–C.
- The agonist muscle creating the movement is the triceps brachii.
- The muscular contraction in the triceps brachii to produce extension at the elbow is concentric.

The shoulder girdle joint
- The articulating bones in the shoulder girdle are the scapula and clavicle.
- The movements produced are elevation and upward rotation from stages A–C. This enables the ball to be lifted up over the head in preparation for it to be thrown up and forwards.
- The agonist muscles which produce the movement in the shoulder girdle are the trapezius (elevation) and the trapezius (upward rotation).
- The muscular contraction in the trapezius is concentric.

The wrist joint
- Articulating bones in the wrist joint are the carpals, radius and ulna.
- The movement produced is supination to pronation, which enables the ball to be thrown forward through stages A–C.
- The agonist muscle in the wrist joint is the pronator teres.
- The types of muscular contraction produced in the pronator

Unit 3: Applied Sport and Exercise Psychology

Relate your learning to a sports and exercise context (pages 63–64)

The completed table is shown below.

Individual's performance	Psychological factors	Possible theories /interventions
Emily: 23-year-old rugby player; recently selected for the Women's England Rugby Team.	Rugby requires positive aggression to be successful	Bandura's social learning theory
Loves competing for the country; gets goose bumps every time she puts on an England shirt.	Motivation	Need achievement theory
Known for getting very nervous before a game which at times can show in the first 10 minutes of any match.	Effect of arousal is negative in the first 10 minutes.	Inverted U hypothesis
After the initial phases of the game Emily transforms into a loud, confident, dominant and aggressive player making tackles all over the pitch.	Self confidence	Vealey's Multidimensional model of sport confidence
Relishes the opportunity to beat her opponents	Positive aggression within the laws of the game	Bandura's social learning theory
The feeling that she gets from winning helps to motivate her to train harder and supports her as she builds up to the next competition.	Motivation from her success	Need achievement theory
In a match, Emily is stretchered off with a serious knee injury requiring immediate surgery to re-attach her anterior cruciate ligament (ACL). The injury is serious and requires a lengthy rehabilitation programme. Emily is convinced she will never play rugby again.	Self-efficacy	Bandura's self-efficacy theory
Since being injured, Emily's personality has changed. She has become argumentative and gets frustrated easily. Eight weeks on, Emily has withdrawn from social situations choosing to stay at home.	Learned helplessness	Dweck's theory
She relies on social media to keep up to date with what is going on and sees that her team mates have been selected to participate in the Olympics. Emily is upset, angry and annoyed that nobody told her directly. She talks with her physiotherapist and realises she has withdrawn from her team mates despite them trying to include her.	Hostile aggression	Bandura's social learning theory
Emily realises the significant physiological and psychological effect of the injury, resulting in negative thought processes that prevent her getting better physically. She learns that through hard work she could play rugby again, which improves her outlook on her injury and develops a 'can do' attitude. Sixteen weeks on, Emily returns to training, feeling excited yet nervous about seeing everyone.	Self-efficacy Motivation	Bandura's self-efficacy theory Need achievement theory
At training, she discusses her feelings with the coach who suggests she may benefit from some psychology support.		Possible interventions: Positive self-talk Positive statements Progressive muscular relaxation Breathing control Imagery Pep talks Goal setting Performance profiling

Consider psychological theories in relation to psychological factors (pages 65–67)

Individual responses that may include the following points.

Theory: Inverted U hypothesis
- States that there is an optimum level of arousal to enhance sport performance.
- When arousal is too low or too high, performance levels are lower.

Psychological factor: Arousal
- Self-regulation of arousal levels is a key characteristic of successful sports performers.
- It is clear that, prior to competing, Emily is in a state of increased arousal, demonstrated by the feeling of nervousness, goosebumps and physiological effects.
- Initially, the level of arousal has a negative impact on Emily's performance in the first 10 mins so the theory supports the findings that she is over aroused at the beginning of the game.
- Then, her arousal affects her performance positively as the game continues. Self-regulation of arousal will be important for Emily to establish when she returns to the game.

Theory: Vealey's multidimensional model of sport confidence
- Suggests that there are key areas that need to be fulfilled to promote self-confidence.
- Factors such as previous success, personality types and skill sets assist in improving self-confidence. The theory relies on being able to recognise what someone is good at and using that to their advantage. Within an elite level team sport, there are a number of self-confidence sources, e.g. from professionals, teammates and supporters.

Psychological factor: Self-confidence
- High levels of self-confidence are key characteristics of successful sports performers. It is important that Emily is self-confident in rugby due to demands of the game.
- Emily displays high confidence generated by experiences in training and competition with a positive impact on performance prior to injury.
- Significant personality changes seen between on and off field, and post-injury, with a negative impact on Emily's self-confidence. Addressing other psychological factors related to the injury will improve self-confidence as a by-product.

Theory: Bandura's social learning theory
- Explains that aggression is a behaviour which is learned by observing others and experiencing reinforcement for eliciting these behaviours.
- The reinforcement can be from anyone and commonly takes the form of praise. This practice is common in sport performers.

Psychological factor: Aggression
- Instrumental, controlled aggression is important for Emily for successful performance in rugby.
- Emily's aggression is suitable, being used to make tackles and to physically compete.

Theory: Bandura's self-efficacy theory
- Suggests that an individual's beliefs about their capabilities to complete a task have a profound effect as to whether they are successful or not.
- The theory explains that there are four sources of self-efficacy. These include mastery experience, various experiences, verbal persuasion and social and emotional influences.

Psychological factor: self-efficacy
- Positive thinking is a key characteristic of successful sports performers. Self-efficacy is closely linked to self-confidence.
- Emily's self-efficacy is initially positive, although she is nervous in the first 10 minutes. It is then impacted negatively with the belief that she will not return to rugby after her injury. Self-efficacy can link to lack of self-esteem that can result in exercise avoidance. The effect of self-efficacy on her rehabilitation will be significant if the negative mindset is not challenged, so this is high priority.

Theory: Dweck's theory
- Argues that people have either a fixed or growth mindset. A fixed mindset is where people believe that particular attributes are fixed in stone, which can lead to learned helplessness. Athletes in this category tend to feel the need to prove themselves continually.
- In contrast, a growth mindset is the 'I will succeed' approach. Athletes who possess this mindset thrive in a challenge and adversity and are willing to adapt to be the best they can.

Psychological factor: Learned helplessness
- Emily feels as if she has failed because of the impact of the injury, and experiences a loss of control that affects her negatively. Learned helplessness has a high impact on injury sufferers and can generate a self-fulfilling prophecy.
- Dweck's theory suggests that rehabilitation can take longer in cases such as Emily's as the individual is unable to help themselves get better. This in turn increases an athlete's anxiety and self-esteem.
- To assist Emily in getting better and returning to playing rugby, it is important to address this issue. Emily's self-efficacy needs to be challenged as a priority if rehabilitation is going to be successful.

Consider psychological interventions (pages 68–70)

Individual responses that might include the following points:

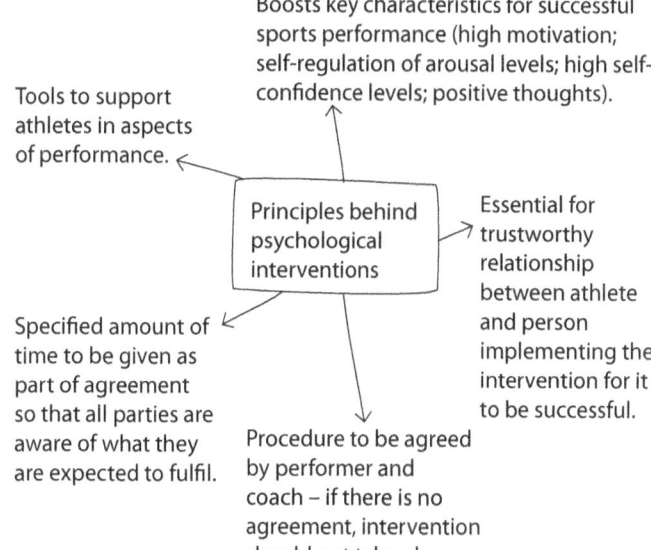

Recommended psychological interventions

Individual responses, relating to Emily's situation, as in the example table below. Notes should suggest the interventions that would be a priority for Emily and why, bearing in mind the need to initially address learned helplessness and self-efficacy as a result of injury, then the psychological factors that will restore Emily to training and successful performance.

Intervention	How implemented	Justification
Positive self-talk, useful for Emily's: • Learned helplessness • Self-confidence • Arousal • Aggression	Used to produce a 'can do' attitude. Involves statements such as 'you can do this' or 'keep going'. It does not use task specific instructions. Cue words or phrases can also be used to help refocus or highlight key elements.	Significant impact on an individual's mind set; it is important that self-talk is used to turn negative thought patterns associated with long-term injuries into positive ones.
Positive statements, useful for Emily's: • Learned helplessness • Self-efficacy	Series of phrases or sentences that can be said to an athlete. Statements used are personal to them, short, clear and simple. Emotive words are also used as part of the statement to enhance self-belief.	Leads to supporting a successful performance linked to injury recovery
Goal setting, useful for Emily's: • Learned helplessness • Motivation • Self-confidence	Key component that keeps athlete focused on specific areas for improvement; goals are often categorised into short, medium and long term highlighting the various durations needed between setting and completing; short-term goals can bring quick success and increase motivation levels; short and medium-term goals makes progress to long-term goals seem more achievable.	Crucial for the final stages of rehabilitation that Emily is focused and positive about moving forward. Can be used to refocus an athlete, concentrating on the here and now or the near future and re-motivate them into achieving, performing and succeeding. Acts as a progress measure. Regularly used to assist an athlete's confidence when returning from injury through achieving small targets.
Imagery, useful for Emily's: • Self-efficacy • Arousal • Self confidence • Aggression	Creates pictures in the mind for each individual aspect of a skill along with the emotions that are commonly felt as part of the activity, without physically completing the skill. Uses visual, auditory and kinaesthetic senses for imagery to be most effective. The principles allow skills to be broken down into small parts and then built back up. Used to create a growth mindset.	Assists with rehabilitation and self-efficacy, helping to influence self-confidence and keep the 'I can do' attitude; reduces anxiety. Further along in recovery, assists in arousal with mental preparation prior to performance and a reinforcement technique. Can be used to build self-confidence in a warm up routine and reduce arousal to its optimum point where it does not affect performance.
Pep talks, useful for Emily's self-efficacy	Most effective from people who the athlete has a good relationship with. Emotive language assists the athlete to believe in themselves and their abilities.	Provides a boost to the athlete; designed to create feelings of self-belief.
Progressive muscular relaxation (PMR), useful for Emily's: • Arousal • Aggression	Relaxes muscle tension in an athlete who is over-aroused/anxious.	Avoids increased muscle tension which reduces the flexibility in muscles, creating a decrease in their range of movement; exposure creates awareness of muscle tension; difficult to use PMR during a sporting situation.
Breathing control, useful for Emily's: • Arousal • Aggression	Relaxes and restores an athlete to a regular breathing pattern where an athlete is over-aroused/anxious so feeling an increase in perceived pressure within sporting situations which alters their breathing pattern.	Controls arousal levels. Can be used to create a positive mindset supported by imagery to reduce the negative effect within the first 10 minutes. Also controls arousal levels which are closely linked to aggression; can be used to increase and decrease arousal, to achieve desired behaviour.
Performance profiling, useful for Emily's motivation.	Breaks down requirements of sport and attributes for successful performance, agreed by coach and player. Athlete and coach score athlete on 1–10 scale for how good they think they are with each attribute, then discuss results and major differences. Information is used as a motivation tool and to set realistic goals.	Used in final stages of rehabilitation, to increase motivation in exercise programmes and performance. Important that it is included as part of recovery; needs to be executed effectively or it could have a detrimental effect on the anticipated outcome

Revision questions

Revision question 1 (pages 72–76)

Individual responses, that may include the following points.

Motivation:
- affects Emily's performance positively with high intrinsic motivation
- Emily's high motivation gives her drive to succeed nationally with a place on the national circuit
- enjoys feeling when wins – sense of pride and achievement; as she is intrinsically motivated, winning matches assist in getting her ready for the next match.
- injury decreases motivation, characterised by convincing herself she won't play rugby again and becoming isolated from social situations
- motivation develops again through physiotherapy intervention, returning to position of excitement in returning to game
- essential that Emily is highly motivated so that she can continue with her rehabilitation programme and return to successful performance.

Self-confidence:
- self-confidence affects Emily positively prior to injury
- essential for rugby; confidence to challenge the opposition
- decline seen post-injury; withdrawal from social situations; feelings expressed in physiotherapy session
- physiotherapy session leads to developing a 'can do' attitude which needs increasing for rehabilitation.

Aggression:
- aggression is a positive psychological factor for Emily prior to injury – controlled aggression instrumental to success; desire to beat opponent within the laws of the game
- changes to hostile aggression when injury is sustained; links to feeling frustrated after becoming injured
- discussion in physiotherapy is a turning point for positive engagement; Emily needs to regain the position of controlled aggression prior to injury.

Arousal:
- negative impact that decreases performance in first 10 minutes, linked to over-arousal, then settles down
- attentional focus could be reduced as Emily makes tackles all over the field; could be argued that this is an unstructured response as she tries to do too much creating a poor performance in the early stages
- needs to develop use of arousal for optimum effect when returning to training.

Self-efficacy:
- Emily's self-efficacy is strong initially as she has self-belief and confidence though this is mixed with nervousness and unsettled early performance
- impacts negatively on Emily after injury; she believes she won't get better and forms negative outlook; behaviour changes with Emily withdrawing from others
- turning point with physiotherapist/advice from others; installs a change in perception; anxiety displayed when returning to the team; feelings identified
- leads to developing a 'can do' attitude which needs increasing for rehabilitation.

Learned helplessness:
- learned helplessness is having the most significant negative effect on Emily
- initially Emily is in a strong and confident position, with drive and motivation
- post-injury Emily shows a fixed mindset with negative thought processes; there is a decrease in self-esteem and an increase in anxiety; she feels sorry for herself and convinces herself she won't get better or play again; she has feelings of failure and isolation due to the injury and seeing the success of her team mates being selected for Olympics; inhibits effective rehabilitation
- changed perception following discussion with physiotherapist bringing about changes to feelings of control and direction that need to be built on for recovery.

Priorities for the significance of each factor

Individual responses. One interpretation of priorities for the significance of each psychological factor to build Emily's performance is given as an example, below.

The highest priority for Emily should be reducing the effect that **learned helplessness** is having on her during her rehabilitation stages.
- This is because learned helplessness will inhibit Emily's ability to be able to get better.
- The impact of learned helplessness on performance is to delay return to sport with potential to also reduce exercise. Emily needs to improve her mental wellbeing, complete her rehabilitation exercises and return to playing.
- By making this a priority, it will assist Emily by empowering her through appropriate interventions to focus on solving the problem rather than telling herself that she will not get better.

A further high priority should be **self-efficacy**.
- This is because Emily is experiencing behaviour changes, withdrawing from others, and believes she won't get better.
- The impact this has on performance is negative as Emily believes she won't get better after her injury and forms an outlook that will inhibit recovery.
- By making this a priority, it will assist Emily by installing a change in perception, helping her to return to the team by introducing a 'can do' attitude.

A medium priority should be **motivation**.
- This is because Emily needs to be motivated to return to the game and recover from her injury; this will also take place as a by-product of addressing learned helplessness and self-efficacy.
- The impact this has on performance is currently negative as injury decreases motivation, characterised by Emily convincing herself she won't play rugby again; extent of this leads to her becoming withdrawn from social situations.
- By making this a priority, it will assist Emily by increasing the likelihood of a successful rehabilitation programme, making her return to rugby more likely to be successful.

A further medium priority should be **self-confidence**.
- This is because Emily needs self-confidence to succeed in rugby when tackling her opponents and in relation to her team mates. Her confidence will also build up as a by-product of addressing learned helplessness and self-efficacy. This will become a higher priority as Emily starts to play in matches again.

- The impact this has on performance is currently negative with a decline post-injury and withdrawal from social situations, as expressed in the physiotherapy session.
- By making this a priority, it will assist Emily by developing a positive attitude about her own abilities and relationships with others, which is needed for a successful rehabilitation programme and strong return to the game.

A lower priority should be **arousal**.
- This is because the focus on arousal is effective when Emily is closer to a return to matches and higher priorities have been addressed.
- The impact this has on performance is currently negative initially, as Emily's: unstructured response leads to poor performance within the first 10 minutes. After the initial stages of the game, Emily settles.
- By making this a priority, it will assist Emily by enabling her to be more effective when she does return to playing.

A further lower priority should be **aggression**.
- This is because in performance, Emily's aggression is appropriate; in injury and recovery, addressing the higher priority factors will reduce her frustrated aggression.
- The impact this has on performance is positive for Emily as controlled aggression is needed in rugby for successful performance.
- By making this a priority, it will assist Emily by addressing her frustration in recovery and supporting her to continue with her controlled aggression when she returns to the field.

Conclusion
- It can be argued that a number of psychological factors have a positive and/or negative impact on Emily's mental wellbeing and performance in rugby.
- The impact these factors have on performance varies greatly and yet a number are entwined. Emily needs to identify and prioritise correctly to ensure rapid and sustained progress.
- The key priorities for improvement and factors demonstrated as having the most significant effect are learned helplessness and self-efficacy. Addressing these will prevent Emily from withdrawing from her rehabilitation programme. If they are not addressed, it is probable that Emily will not recover. If they are addressed, it is highly probable that Emily will successfully return to rugby, benefiting from having also addressed a range of psychological factors.

Revision question 2 (pages 77–81)

Individual responses. The following points may be included, reflecting one interpretation of how psychological theories can account for Emily's experiences, as an example.

Need achievement theory
- Psychological factor: motivation; the level of motivation has a significant impact on performance.
- Psychological theory: need achievement theory accounts for Emily's intrinsic motivation. Suggests that all athletes can be grouped into two categories: the need to achieve and the need to avoid failure. The model can be applied to any situation or individual.
- Athletes who need to achieve:
  - strive for success
  - keep going when things go wrong
  - feel a sense of pride in accomplishments.
- Prior to injury: Emily demonstrates 'need to achieve' factors – she uses feelings of winning to enhance performance; her level of motivation affects her ability to perform; there are links to over-motivation, and links to arousal.
- After injury: recognised that characteristics of an individual may change in response to a situation, so 'need to achieve position' may change to 'need to avoid failure'. In Emily's case, it could be argued that the need to avoid failure will have a significant influence on her return as she will not want to become injured again. This will need careful management, with the need for good interventions to be utilised, to ensure that she is ready to return to playing rugby.

- During the recovery phase, the 'need to achieve' will be applied, supporting Emily with a successful return. This phase will include an element of things not going right; however, Emily will be motivated through the achievements in the recovery phase. It is important that people who matter to Emily elicit motivated behaviour from her to support her in becoming the best rugby player she can be.
- This clearly demonstrates that the 'need to achieve theory' is relevant to Emily because it is a diverse theory that can be applied to Emily's experiences, ranging from being fit to play through to return to the game.

Vealey's multidimensional model

- Psychological factor: self-confidence; needed because it is an essential characteristic for a successful rugby player. At elite level, it is fundamentally important for an athlete to have self-confidence to enable them to make tackles knowing that they have the necessary skills to be effective and prevent their opponent scoring a try.
- Psychological theory: Vealey's multidimensional model of sport confidence is relevant to Emily when assessing her level of self-confidence throughout her experiences.
- This model explains that self-confidence can change based on a series of factors. Injury can be classified in the personal factor section of the model which shows that when personal factors change there is an effect on self-confidence. The model suggests there are a number of people who can affect an individual's self-confidence; key people are those who have a close relationship with the athlete; the greater the self-confidence, the better the performance.
- Prior to injury: Emily displays self-confidence.
- After injury: Emily's self-confidence is lowered, resulting in withdrawal from social situations; decrease in self-confidence contributes to negative thought processes and beliefs; shows how quickly self-confidence can be lost. Links with Dweck's theory where the athlete's mindset plays an important part on, on for example, how much of an effect others have on their self-confidence.
- Recovery: the role of the physiotherapist and psychologist includes emotional support through encouraging Emily by using positive reinforcement. It is likely that the psychologist would use positive statements with Emily to support her development. The role of the coach will also be key in the process to help Emily return to the squad. The coach will work with the psychologist to ensure the transition back into the team is carefully managed and that any anxiety perceived by Emily is considered and reduced where possible.

Bandura's social learning theory

- Psychological factor: instrumental aggression (prior to injury) – the type of aggression needed for rugby; hostile aggression (after injury).
- Psychological theory: Bandura's social learning theory, due to the level of controlled aggression being used initially. It would be reinforced by the coach, team mates and others. Key components of social learning theory are that aggression is learned through watching others; praise is given by others when aggression has been used correctly; this acts as an example.
- Prior to injury: Emily plays with appropriate levels of aggression ensuring that she is a successful player.
- After injury: the aggression type changes from instrumental aggression to hostile aggression. Hostile aggression is shown as Emily became frustrated with the injury situation. It is likely at this point that she will replay the last few moments prior to becoming injured and what it was like the moments afterwards. Additionally, feelings of 'why me?' are likely to occur. The level of hostile aggression will increase if the team continues to be successful without her or if she perceives the process to recovery as being slow.
- Recovery: through the recovery process Emily will have moments where she feels highly frustrated which will increase hostile aggression levels. However, the physiotherapist/coach/psychologist will support Emily to reduce these feelings and assist her to use them in a positive way, moving back to instrumental aggression in a way that aligns with Bandura's social learning theory.

Inverted U hypothesis

- Psychological factor: arousal.
- Psychological theory: inverted U hypothesis. This explains that there is an optimum level of arousal which supports optimum performance. If arousal is too high or too low, then psychological and physiological responses occur, causing a change in performance. The decrease in Emily's performance demonstrates both physical and psychological arousal. Performance improves as time progresses, therefore it cannot be linked to catastrophe theory as this suggests that once arousal levels go too high the performance is poor. The inverted U hypothesis explains that performance levels can change as arousal increases and decreases.
- Prior to injury: this theory can be found in Emily's case due to the transitional changes that occur after the first 10 minutes of the game, where arousal levels are high and it takes 10 minutes for Emily to settle in to her performance. Emily is running around making tackles all over the field which shows her confidence and may also show a common effect of reduction in attentional focus creating an uncontrolled start. Emily controls arousal after initial stages, settling in to the game.
- After injury: increased arousal is seen when returning to training.
- Recovery: this theory can be applied within the recovery process as the athlete pushes themselves to get better. However, this must be carefully managed to ensure there is no further damage. When Emily gets the opportunity to begin light training she will be highly aroused so it will be important that she has the techniques to reduce the effect this will have on her performance.

Bandura's self-efficacy theory

- Psychological factor: self-efficacy.
- Psychological theory: self-efficacy is a person's belief that they can do something successfully. The theory that relates to this is Bandura's self-efficacy theory. The theory explains that when there are changes in emotional and psychological states, self-efficacy occurs. The model direction can move self-efficacy from high to low depending on the situational changes in psychological states.
- Prior to injury: Emily is clearly focused on performance and winning; looks to possess self-confidence, self-esteem, arousal and motivation.
- After injury: low position demonstrated; Emily tells herself that she won't get better, leading to a decline in time with team mates and isolation. There is a substantial change in her psychological and emotional state resulting in a change in her self-efficacy.
- Recovery: within the recovery phase, Bandura's self-efficacy model can be applied. Emily adapts from a low position to a higher position as she prepares to return to the team. Changes in self-efficacy are shown as she becomes more engaged with others and make progress with her recovery phase.

Dweck's theory of learned helplessness

- Psychological factor: learned helplessness, where athletes believe that a situation is outside of their control, so give up easily.
- Psychological theory: Dweck's theory of learned helplessness. The theory explains that there are 'fixed' and 'growth' mindsets. When athletes have learned helplessness and believe a situation is outside of their control, they give up easily as they can't see how to make the situation better. They may avoid certain situations, choose unachievable tasks to give them an excuse for failure and be less likely to solve problems, which may lead to a reduced performance level. This theory is key for Emily as she moves from a growth mindset to negative thought processes occurring with a significant impact on self-efficacy and confidence.
- Prior to injury: Emily displays a growth mindset using performance outcomes to support her with preparation to the next performance.

- After injury: Emily changes to a fixed mindset; she convinces herself that she will not get better; demonstrates an increase in aggression.
- Recovery: Emily moves back to a growth mindset following the changes in the injury phases and following professional help through the physiotherapy session, assisting her to believe she can get better.

Conclusion
- A number of different psychological theories can be applied to the psychological factors impacting on Emily and her performance. The importance of Emily responding positively in the context of the factors and theories, alongside prioritising interventions, will be critical to her recovery.

Revision question 3 (pages 82–88)

Individual responses. The following points may be included, reflecting one interpretation of possible interventions to meet Emily's needs, as an example.

Pyschological interventions
- Pyschological interventions are tools to support athletes in aspects of performance. A number of interventions could be used to enhance Emily's state of mind and her performance in relation to the identified psychological factors following her injury.
- For psychological interventions to be successful, a number of principles need to be fulfilled.
- A trustworthy relationship between athlete and person implementing the intervention is essential if it is to be successful.
- Procedure should be agreed by the performer and the coach – if there is no agreement then the intervention should not take place.
- Recommended that, as part of the agreement, a specified amount of time is given so that all parties are aware of what they are expected to fulfil.

Positive self-talk
- How does it work/what does it improve? Involves talking to oneself in a positive manner about themselves. Commonly it is non-verbalised dialogue. The process involves changing negative thoughts into positive ones, i.e. from 'I can't do this' to 'I'm finding this challenging but I'm going to persevere and give it my best'.
- Why is it needed? Recommended to assist Emily in relation to improving the impact of the psychological factors of learned helplessness, self-confidence, arousal and aggression.
- Application to Emily: Following the injury, this intervention could become part of Emily's immediate rehabilitation progress. She could use it to adapt negative thoughts into positive thought processes, especially for learned helplessness which is common in elite level players particularly when their injury is serious and requires a lengthy rehabilitation programme.
- Implementation: Having built in self-talk to support Emily with her rehabilitation it could then be transferred into her sporting performances.
- Justification and priority: This is a high priority for Emily as it will enable her to challenge negative thought processes leading to a growth mindset. It will provide Emily with the tools to be able to manage challenging situations effectively as the process is solution-directed. The psychological factors recommended for this intervention for Emily include learned helplessness which is a high priority for Emily. It is essential that the negative thoughts she experiences are addressed and the 'I can do' attitude is restored quickly.

Goal setting
- How does it work/what does it improve? Used to assist an athlete to remain focused. Goals are categorised into short, medium and long term. It is important to highlight the differences needed in the duration between setting them and completing them.
- Why is it needed? Recommended to assist Emily in relation to the psychological factors of learned helplessness, motivation, self-confidence.
- Application to Emily: In Emily's case, goal setting is crucial to enable her to see improvements over a relatively short period of time as she adjusts to injury and recovery. It is important that goal setting is progressive and coherent, allowing short- and medium-term goals to build into the established long-term goal.
- Implementation: Emily needs a high number of short-term goals to enable her to obtain quick successes to keep her motivated to continue to improve. When Emily returns from injury, medium- and long-term goals will become increasingly important.
- Justification and priority: Goal setting is a high priority and works best for athletes who are intrinsically motivated, or those who are driven by targets. This is needed to enhance the motivation levels of Emily to assist her to improve. It also supports a change in mindset, outlined in Dweck's theory, as she reverts back into a growth mindset as opposed to a fixed one. The psychological factors recommended for this intervention for Emily include learned helplessness, a high priority for Emily. Immediate short-term goals need to be established with Emily by the physiotherapist/psychologist/coach to assist her with her rehabilitation.

Positive statements
- How does it work/what does it improve? These consist of a series of statements that can be read by or said to an athlete. As a process changes, so too can the statements in order to reflect this change in situation. The statements are individual to the athlete and are designed to reduce the learned helplessness effect by enhancing the athlete's emotional state.
- Why is it needed? Recommended for Emily's learned helplessness, self-efficacy.
- Application to Emily: Clear from that Emily has got into a cycle of negative thought processes. Positive statements are needed to help retrain Emily's brain to be supportive of her situation but not allow herself to opt out of getting better.
- Implementation: Quick to use and design, ready to use immediately. If used regularly, it will have a quick improvement on Emily's wellbeing.
- Justification and priority: Positive statements are a high priority for Emily as they are needed to promote a can-do attitude. The psychological factors recommended for this intervention for Emily include learned helplessness and self-efficacy – high priorities for Emily.

Imagery
- How does it work/what does it improve? Imagery involves creating an image or series of images in the mind along with emotions that are associated with the activity or skill. Effective imagery should use visual, auditory and kinaesthetic senses. This intervention does not require the athlete to physically conduct the activity but to psychologically replay the activity in their head, focusing on different aspects to improve.
- Why is it needed? Recommended to improve Emily's self-efficacy, self-confidence, arousal and aggression.
- Application to Emily: This tool will especially help to boost Emily's self-efficacy and self-confidence, re-installing an 'I can do' attitude. It will also help direct Emily's arousal and aggression.
- Implementation: Imagery as a skill can take a while to master correctly. Therefore, time is needed to ensure that Emily is able to complete it successfully, at first with support and then independently. This can then be transferred from part of the rehabilitation programme to a performance routine and then be used to help reduce the effect of high levels of arousal that Emily experiences prior to competition.
- Justification and priority: Imageryis a high priority for Emily as it is a useful intervention particularly when an athlete is returning from injury. The psychological factors recommended for this intervention for Emily include self-efficacy – a high priority for Emily.

Pep talks
- How does it work/what does it improve? Most effective when conducted by people who have the respect of the athlete and a good relationship with them. Pep talks are individual and often

do not follow a script so the content of the talk can change significantly between each intervention to target specific points for improvement.
- Why is it needed? Recommended to improve Emily's self-efficacy.
- Application to Emily: It is important that pep talks are used to assist Emily with her transition back from injury to fitness.
- Implementation: To be used regularly for a significant impact on Emily's self-efficacy.
- Justification and priority: pep talks are a high priority for Emily because it is important that they are used to boost Emily's beliefs about what she can achieve. The psychological factors recommended for this intervention for Emily include self-efficacy, which is a high priority for Emily.

Progressive muscular relaxation
- How does it work/what does it improve? Progressive muscular relaxation (PMR) is used commonly as a relaxation tool. The process of the technique requires the athlete to recognise that there is an increase in muscle tension and, through a prescribed process, loosen the muscle/muscle groups, one at a time.
- Why is it needed? Recommended for Emily's arousal, aggression.
- Application to Emily: PMR could be used to reduce the level of aggression experienced by Emily since she has become injured and to help manage her arousal.
- Implementation: PMR is a useful tool as part of a pre-performance routine or within day-to-day life. However, it is not possible to apply this process whilst competing due to the length of time that it takes to perform.
- Justification and priority: This intervention has a lower overall priority for Emily at this stage, as higher priority interventions may reduce the need for this intervention. It could act in a complementary way. PMR is most effective when an individual is over-aroused or anxious. When over-arousal occurs, there's a significant increase in muscle tension which decreases the range of movement in a muscle. This will have a significant effect on Emily's performance as she may not be able to throw or kick the ball as far as she might within a training situation. By using this technique, Emily would become able to recognise when tension was building in the muscles. The technique is also useful in reducing the effect aggression has in the body.

Breathing control
- How does it work/what does it improve? The technique requires the athlete to relax through a series of breathing exercises which can assist in reducing aggressive outbursts and also levels of anxiety. The technique is are quick and easy to use and apply.
- Why is it needed? Recommended for Emily's arousal, aggression.
- Application to Emily: Used to control arousal and aggression levels in athletes. It may be effective when Emily is competing again and she needs to regain control of her emotions.
- Implementation: This intervention can be used at any point as it is quick to teach Emily what she needs to do. It can be used as part of day-to-day life as well as in competition.
- Justification and priority: This is a lower overall priority for Emily at this stage, as the higher priority interventions may reduce the need for this intervention. It could act in a complementary way. It can be applied to Emily due to the increasing levels of frustration and aggression seen since she has become injured. The change from instrumental to hostile aggression has been identified. The technique can be deployed to prevent aggressive outbursts when she is feeling most frustrated.

Performance profiling
- How does it work/what does it improve? The technique is used between athletes and their coach or sports psychologist and breaks down the key components of the sport, assessing what is needed for a successful sports performance. The athlete then rates themselves against the criteria and the coach does the same. Both parties then meet to discuss the outcome of the exercise. Information is then used to support goal-setting to assist with improving areas that are considered important for development.
- Why is it needed? Recommended to enhance Emily's motivation.
- Application to Emily: Useful tool for someone who is returning from injury or needs an increase in motivation. This would be useful in Emily's case to assist her with her return to training and performance as it can focus her and her coaches' attention on what needs to be improved.
- Implementation: The return from injury is a good time to do this because it can be used as part of Emily's phased return in the final stages of the rehabilitation programme, so she can focus on what was working well prior to the injury and what needed improving. Injury period has provided a good point to review progress.
- Justification and priority: This is a lower overall priority for Emily because it is part of a long-term strategy to support Emily's performance development. It is recommended that this intervention is only started once Emily has returned to training – the last intervention to be implemented.

Conclusion
- A number of interventions are recommended for use by Emily and her coach to assist her in returning from injury, recovering mentally and enhancing her performance.
- The outline of interventions demonstrates the impact they would have on Emily as an individual and for her performance.
- The key findings suggest that priority interventions are goal setting, positive statement and self-talk. This is because these three interventions can be used to support and improve other psychological factors without the athlete needing to spend lots of time completing an array of routines. By prioritising the interventions, Emily can focus her efforts without compromising her recovery.

Unit 13: Nutrition for Sport and Exercise Performance

Relate your learning to a sports and exercise context (pages 91–93)

Nutritional programme
Example answers:
1. Olivia has a varied range of intakes, particularly for energy and fluid.
2. Seems to be very consistent with breakfast choices.
3. Could snacks be replaced with better options?
4. Greater fluid intake needs to be considered.
5. The individual may have a high training day on Tuesday.
6. The individual may be having a rest day on Thursday.
7. No sports food or supplements are currently included in the nutritional programme and the benefits could be considered.
8. Initially, it would be useful to:
   a) add up the macronutrient and energy values and work out the average intake for the typical seven-day period
   b) work out the key nutrients supplied in the breakfast choices
   c) take into account when the individual consumes her snacks.

Personal and performance details
Example answers:
1. Breakfast was consumed at least 3 hours before training which should have allowed for optimal glycogen stores and adequate hydration. Lunch was consumed within 2 hours to replenish muscle glycogen stores
2. Monday has low fluid intake for a training day.
3. Tuesday is probably a hard session. Energy, carbohydrate and fluid intakes reflect this, as they are the highest intakes consumed throughout the week.
4. Despite this being a rest day, it would be beneficial to achieve a higher fluid intake.
5. Although there is a high fluid intake, carbohydrate is below the lower end of the intake target. There is a lower than calculated overall energy intake, probably reflective of a non-training day.

6. Carbohydrate intake is below the lower end of target intake and overall energy intake is below target requirement, but fluid intake is high.
7. Carbohydrate intake is towards the upper end of intake target and just above energy intake target.
8. The nutritional preparation will need to be modified to reflect the training and pre-, during and post-event nutritional requirements.

Nutrition for health and wellbeing (pages 94–99)

Individual notes that should reflect the following factors.

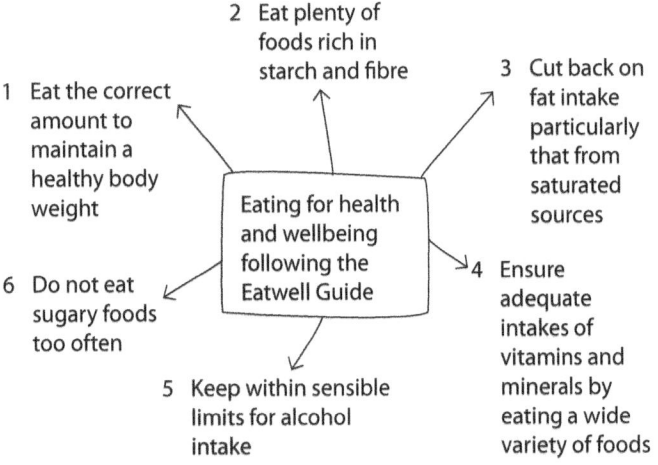

1. Eat the correct amount to maintain a healthy body weight
2. Eat plenty of foods rich in starch and fibre
3. Cut back on fat intake particularly that from saturated sources
4. Ensure adequate intakes of vitamins and minerals by eating a wide variety of foods
5. Keep within sensible limits for alcohol intake
6. Do not eat sugary foods too often

Eating for health and wellbeing following the Eatwell Guide

Estimating energy requirements (pages 94-95)
Individual responses, using the Harris-Benedict equation for calculating BMR and PALS in males.

Interpreting Olivia's energy intake from the nutrition programme (page 95)
- The range of energy intake shown is from to 2180 to 3090.
- The intake might fluctuate to match the needs of her training schedule – the lowest days are Friday and Monday. The higher days are Tuesday and Thursday.
- Her average daily energy intake, adding all values up and dividing by 7 is 2548 kcal.

Interpreting Olivia's carbohydrate intake from the nutrition programme (page 96)
- Calculating Olivia's carbohydrate intake over the seven days her average daily carbohydrate intake is 333 g.
- The range of intakes is from 275 g to 385 g.

Estimating protein requirements (page 96)
Daily protein requirements based on type of activity:

Type of activity	Protein per kg of body weight (g)
Mainly endurance	1.2–1.4
Mainly strength	1.2–1.7

Interpreting Olivia's protein intake from the nutrition programme (page 96)
- Olivia's protein intake ranges from 75 to 110 g.

Interpreting Olivia's fat intake from the nutrition programme (page 97)
- In considering Olivia's fat intake, her range of intakes is from 80 to 130 g, with an average intake of 94 g per day.
- This is slightly above the guidelines for the sedentary population for females.

Interpreting Olivia's calcium and iron intake from the nutrition programme (page 97)
- As a female athlete, Olivia should be encouraged to consume an adequate calcium and iron intake. In the current intake, rich sources of these are cheese, milk, milkshake and cabbage (calcium) and beef, pork, chicken and peas (iron).

Estimating fluid requirements (page 97)
For an athlete weighing 57 kg using formula A:
$30 \times 57 = 1710$ ml
$35 \times 57 = 1995$ ml

Using formula B:
1 ml per calorie of energy requirement would be 2478 ml

Interpreting Olivia's fluid requirements (page 97)
- I can see from Olivia's current nutritional intake that her fluid intake is quite inconsistent ranging from 1100 to 3955 ml. It would be useful to consider what might be impacting on that.
- When evaluating details of her training programme, her high intake days can be variable in relation to her expenditure.
- Her average intake is 2384 ml per day.
- In assessing the adequacy of Olivia's fluid intake, it would also be helpful to consider the quality of her fluid choices and that she is likely to need additional fluid if competing or training in the heat.

Interpreting Olivia's nutritional programme with reference to digestion and absorption (page 98)
Before the body can make use of the energy and nutrients that food contains, it has to be broken down through the processes of digestion and absorption. The precise timing of this depends upon the food which has been eaten and complexity of its structure. This also varies from person to person, but overall:
- it usually takes 6–8 hours for food to pass through the stomach and small intestine
- carbohydrates are digested quickest
- protein takes a bit longer
- fat takes the longest
- slowed by a high fibre content.

Olivia might want to consider the quantity and type of foods and fluids to consume before, during and after exercise to optimise her nutritional strategies around her sport and exercise. This will be affected by the event she is training for and the days on which she trains.

Overview of nutrition programme (page 98-99)
The Eatwell Guide shows the different types of foods and drinks individuals should consume and in what proportions to obtain a healthy, balanced diet. In order to eat in line with the Eatwell Guide, Olivia should aim to:
- Eat at least five portions of a variety of fruit and vegetables every day. Olivia eats between three and five servings per day.
- Base her meals on potatoes, bread, rice, pasta or other starchy carbohydrates. She should choose wholegrain versions where possible. Olivia achieves this at her main meals and sometimes uses breakfast cereals as a snack.
- Have some dairy or dairy alternatives, choosing lower fat and lower sugar options where possible. Olivia consumes between two and three servings per day.
- Eat some beans, pulses, eggs, meat and other proteins (including two portions of fish every week and at least one oily fish.
- Choose unsaturated oils and spreads and consume these in small amounts. It is difficult to tell from Olivia's nutritional programme what types of spreads and oils she uses but some of her snack food choices will be high in fat that might be limiting her overall carbohydrate intake.
- Drink at least six to eight cups/glasses of fluid a day. Olivia's nutritional programme shows low fluid intakes on at least four days out of the seven. It would need to be explored whether this is a reflection of her actual intake or whether she has just forgotten to record it.

- For health, where foods and drinks high in fat, salt or sugar are consumed she should have these less often and in small amounts, or restrict her use of high sugar foods to days when energy expenditure is greatest.

Factors that might be influencing whether Olivia meets her requirements or not, might be related to her nutritional knowledge, the time she has to prepare and eat her food in relation to the time she spends training, where she is when she is eating and the food choices available. If she is not meeting her requirements, she is likely to find training harder and recovery from training less than optimal.

Modifying nutrition for sporting events (pages 100–102)

Information about Olivia's nutrition intake and days where nutrition is needed for training (page 100)

```
        Information on nutrition intake that may
        inform nutritional modifications.
                    /         \
                   /           \
On Tuesday and Sunday,     It would be useful to review
Olivia has milkshake which the quality of Olivia's snacks
links to training days and can and when she consumes them.
be used as a recovery strategy It might be useful to consider
post-training.             introducing sports foods and
                           supplements into Olivia's
                           nutritional programme.
```

Optimising the nutritional programme (page 100)
Individual responses, based on chosen levels of activity and adaptations.

Spidergram of what would need to be considered for nutritional modifications and strategies (page 101)

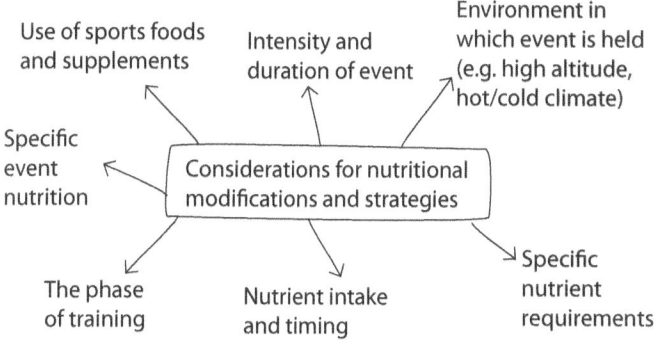

Spidergram of what you expect to be the anticipated outcomes of possible modifications (page 101)
Individual responses, including, for example, better or shorter recovery between sessions; the avoidance of fatigue, illness and injury; stabilised weight; better overall fluid intake and hydration status.

Day's menu plan for adapting a nutritional programme to support optimal performance in training for some selected training events (page 102)
Individual responses depending on choices. General strategies that might be helpful to consider:
- eating a meal or snack 2–4 hours before training to optimise energy available
- eating a carbohydrate-rich snack within the first 30 minutes post-exercise when glycogen resynthesis is at its optimum
- developing a kit bag snack pack of transportable items to kick-start recovery immediately after training
- monitoring hydration status through simple urine colour and volume checks, and ensuring thirst is avoided.

Nutrition intake for different phases of events (pages 103–106)

Guidance on nutrition intake for different phases of training and sports events
Individual responses. Completed diagrams may include, for example:
(page 103)

1. A pre-competition meal should aim to top up muscle and liver glycogen stores. It should be rich in carbohydrate but low in fat and fibre and should contain a moderate amount of protein.

2. Larger meals take longer to digest and nervousness can result in delayed digestion.

Pre-training or event

4. Competition is not a time to experiment with new foods.

3. Olivia should be encouraged to begin fully hydrating and to consume fluids both during and after activity. She can use training as an opportunity to practise hydration strategies. Drinking 300 to 500 ml of fluid 10 to 15 minutes before exercise is recommended.

(page 104)

1. Fluid loss is a major consideration.

2. During intense training or competition isotonic sports drinks may be beneficial especially if training or competition lasts longer than 60 minutes.

During training or event

5. Nutritional challenges during the sporting event will likely relate to avoiding dehydration and ensuring adequate energy along with avoiding gastrointestinal disturbance.

3. During endurance or ultra-endurance events lasting longer than 4 hours, solid foods may be needed. In these instances, energy bars or gels might be useful as a more concentrated source of carbohydrate.

4. Drinking 150 to 200 ml every 15 to 20 minutes during exercise is recommended, especially if the exercise lasts longer than an hour.

(page 104)

Post-training or event

1. Refuel as soon as possible after each training session or event. The longer refuelling is delayed, the longer it will take to fully refuel.
2. A high carbohydrate diet is required. Small, frequent meals and snacks at regular intervals may help to maximise glycogen synthesis.
3. Carbohydrates are preferred that are easy to eat and digest.
4. Consume a high-carbohydrate (at least 50 g) low-fat snack as soon as possible after training or competition, preferably within the first half hour – when the muscles' capacity to refuel is greatest and follow this up with the next meal, which should be rich in carbohydrate, within 2 hours.
5. Rehydration should start immediately. Drinks containing carbohydrates will also assist with energy and glycogen replacement. These may be particularly useful if the activity has been intense and resulted in a suppression of appetite and a reluctance to eat solid foods.
6. Weight and urine-colour checks are a useful and simple way of monitoring fluid status. A weight reduction of 1 kg is equivalent to 1 litre of fluid loss.
7. Fluid losses should be replaced with 1.5 times what was lost, within the first 2 hours of recovery.

Strength and power events

1. Nutritional strategies should support the development and maintenance of lean body mass (muscle) as well as meeting energy needs.
2. Carbohydrate requirements are not as great as they are for endurance events, but are still important.
3. Combining carbohydrate with protein post-exercise promotes an anabolic environment and increases protein synthesis that helps promote muscle development.

Weight-category or weight-controlled events

1. Fewer calories consumed, means fewer nutrients consumed.
2. Calcium and iron intakes are important particularly in the diet of female participants in these sports.
3. Healthy eating and Eatwell Guide principles apply to the planning of dietary intakes for these sports, but greater emphasis may be placed on a low-fat diet.
4. Adequate fluid intake and hydration are essential to maintain concentration for the technical demands of these sports.

Nutritional strategies for different sports and phases – factors to consider (page 105)
Individual responses. Completed diagrams may include, for example:

Endurance events

1. Endurance events challenge energy and fluid stores.
2. Endurance athletes should aim to maximise glycogen stores by increasing carbohydrate intake during the two or three days before competition.
3. Carbohydrate supplements (energy drinks, bars or gels) may be useful.
4. Endurance athletes should start exercise fully hydrated.
5. The longer the duration of the activity, the more important it is to consume fluids during it.
6. Sports drinks can provide carbohydrate as well as replacement of fluids.

Observations for Olivia (page 106)
- Olivia does not currently consume any sports foods or supplements in her nutritional programme
- It would be useful to consider the risks versus benefits of any sports foods or supplements that could be incorporated into Olivia's nutritional strategies pre-, during and post- training or during her event Olivia could consider using energy drinks or gels, protein supplements, caffeine, beetroot juice.

Revision questions

Revision question 1 (pages 107–111)

Individual responses, which may include the following.
To eat for health and wellbeing, Olivia should:
- Eat the correct amount to maintain a healthy body weight and her personal details suggest she is within this range.
- Eat plenty of foods rich in starch and fibre. She tends to base her main meals around these foods. Olivia could swap some cakes and cookies for bagels, toast and more breakfast cereal.
- Cut back on fat intake, particularly saturated sources. Improve some snack food choices to reduce this and provide more carbohydrate in her diet. The higher intake recorded on Tuesday reflects the consumption of chips and chocolate cake.
- Ensure adequate intakes of vitamins and minerals by eating a wide variety of foods. Olivia generally has between three to five servings of fruit and vegetables and two to three servings of dairy foods each day, so both targets for eating for health and wellbeing could be improved.
  As a female endurance athlete, Olivia should ensure she has an adequate intake of calcium and iron.
- Keep within sensible limits for alcohol intake. From the current nutritional intake alcohol is not consumed so this is helpful from a health and performance point of view.

- Not eat sugary foods too often. At times, they may help refuelling and optimal recovery after exercise but intakes need to be considered alongside overall carbohydrate intake and quality of food choices. At the moment, Olivia is using chocolate bars and cookies to boost her carbohydrate intake.

Predicting energy and nutrient requirements for a more detailed interpretation of Olivia's food intake:

- Using the Harris-Benedict equation for calculating BMR and a physical activity factor of 1.725 at 2461 kcal per day.
  BMR = 655.1 + (9.56 × 57) + (1.85 × 168) − (4.68 × 18)
  655.1 + 544.92 + 310.8 − 84.24
  1510.82 − 84.24 = <u>1426.58 kcal</u>
  TER = 1426.58 × 1.725 = <u>2461 kcal</u>
- Some days Olivia is close to meeting this requirement, on others she is either well below or significantly above. However, it is to be expected that her intake will vary, dependent on the exact nature of her training schedule, i.e. her energy requirements will not be exactly the same day in, day out.
- Her average daily energy intake is 2548 kcal, so she is in energy balance and overall consuming enough calories for stable body weight.
- Lowest intake day is the second rest day which you might expect to see, as long as she has fully refuelled on the first rest day
- Highest intake day is Tuesday, probably one of the hardest training days of the week despite only being a single session day, which you would want to see.
- Relatively low intake on Saturday, a double session day, is not so good, achieving only 2340 kcals. Dried fruit consumed after the second training session would help boost energy and carbohydrate intake.

Carbohydrates

- As Olivia's training level is high, requirement for carbohydrate will be high.
- She is training between 45 mins to 2 hours, five days of the week. On training days she is likely to have a carbohydrate requirement of 6–7 g per kilogram of body weight per day:
  6 × 57 = 342 g
  7 × 57 = 399 g
  As a percentage of her overall energy requirement, this would represent 55–65%.
  342 × 4 = 1368
  1368 ÷ 2461 = 0.555
  0.555 × 100 = 56%
  399 × 4 = 1596
  1596 ÷ 2461 = 0.648
  0.648 × 100 = 65%
- Olivia's average carbohydrate intake over the seven days is 333 g with a range of intakes from 275 to 385 g. This might mean that she is not adequately refuelling between all training sessions.
- Looking at her carbohydrate intake more closely, Olivia's highest carbohydrate intake recorded is on Thursday. This helps to restore muscle glycogen stores for the hard training sessions later in the week, particularly on double training days.
- Lowest intake is on the second rest day which might be expected if she has fully refuelled the day before.
- On Saturday where she has two sessions and a hard hills session, Olivia only achieved a carbohydrate intake of 310 g. She is not likely to meet her needs. The hill session may have been particularly hard, affecting appetite afterwards. No milkshake was consumed this day which can be used as a good post-training recovery option to replenish carbohydrate, protein and fluid.

Protein

- As Olivia's sport is endurance focused, her protein requirements are likely to fall in the range of 1.2–1.4 g per kilogram of body weight giving her a target intake of between 68 and 80 g per day.
- Her range of protein intakes is from 75 to 110 g, so she appears to be meeting her protein requirements especially with a source of high biological value protein at each of her main meals.

Fats

- Olivia's fat intake ranges from 80 to 130 g; average intake 94 g per day; slightly above guidelines for healthy fat intake for the sedentary population for females
- When considered as a percentage of her overall calorie intake 655/2548, this represents 26 per cent, in line with eating for health
- It may be helpful for Olivia to replace some fat in her diet with additional carbohydrate to optimise her recovery around training, such as swapping her cakes and cookies for bagels, toast and more breakfast cereal.

Fluids

- Based on using the formula 1 ml per calorie of energy requirement Olivia's fluid requirements would be around 2461 ml per day; environmental conditions should also be taken into account; also specific demands of individual training sessions.
- From current nutritional intake, Olivia's fluid intake is quite inconsistent ranging from 1100 to 3955 ml; consider what might be impacting on this, e.g. poor planning and preparation; under-reporting the intake, as lowest recorded intake was on the first rest day and she may not be as focused on meeting her hydration needs on a rest day; though she did much better on her second rest day, suggesting it may be a reporting error rather than under consumption.
- Olivia is not meeting her fluid intake targets on the days she undertakes her easy runs and it would be recommended that she aims to drink an additional litre of fluid on these days.
- Considering the quality of Olivia's fluid choices, water is considered adequate and suitable for most exercise, but some sports drinks may be useful when exercising at higher intensities for longer duration.
- Olivia does occasionally consume a bottle of vanilla milkshake; it would be helpful to know if she is using this as part of her recovery nutrition strategy on training days to provide protein as well as carbohydrate as part of her immediate post-exercise nutrition strategy.

Factors affecting digestion and absorption of nutrients and fluids

- Before the body can make use of the energy and nutrients that food contains, it has to be broken down through the processes of digestion and absorption.
- The precise timing depends upon the food eaten and complexity of structure and varies for different individuals but for healthy adults it is usually between 24 and 72 hours depending on what has been consumed.
- In general, after eating it takes between 6 to 8 hours for food to pass through the stomach and small intestine.
- Carbohydrates spend the least amount of time in the stomach and are digested quickest. Protein takes a bit longer, whilst fat takes the longest to fully digest. Digestion and absorption are slowed by a high fibre content.
- Many factors can influence the effectiveness of fluid-replacement strategies during and after exercise. Fluid replacement can be accelerated by drinking still, cool drinks of reasonable volume. They should not be too concentrated, and they must be palatable to drink. The more intense the activity, the more the absorption of fluid is slowed.
- Unpleasant symptoms experienced when drinking during exercise usually mean the athlete has started drinking too late and they are already dehydrated.
- Starting exercise well hydrated and keeping a larger fluid volume in the gut also facilitates rehydration as does the inclusion of sodium in the fluids consumed.
- Olivia might want to consider the type, quantity and timing of foods and fluids to consume before, during and after exercise to optimise her nutritional strategies around her sport and training. In considering factors affecting digestion and absorption, it would have been helpful to have known when the fluids and snacks are consumed around training. However, looking at the

timings of her main meals, it does appear that she is leaving a sensible amount of time between eating and training to avoid gastrointestinal discomfort.

Conclusion
- After undertaking a detailed interpretation of Olivia's food and fluid intake with reference to requirements for health and well-being, it is clear that she has a reasonably good diet on which to build more specific nutritional strategies to help her optimise her performance in training and competition.

Revision question 2 (pages 112–115)

Individual responses that may include the following.

Strategies for training
- Olivia is currently training for a cross-country event four weeks away. To optimise training and competition performance, she should consider the timing of her food and fluid intake around pre- and post-training and her event. Good nutritional strategies help to optimise training adaptations and overall recovery. She generally eats 2–3 hours before training and within 2 hours afterwards. Post-exercise carbohydrates that are easy to eat and digest are preferred; often this can be in the form of fluids.

Modifications to improve Olivia's overall intake
- Overall Olivia has a good and varied food intake, but she needs to pay greater attention to increasing her carbohydrate intake on some training days, particularly Saturday where intake falls below predicted ranges of requirements. She can use the Eatwell Guide principles to plan her meals. These principles should form the foundations on which to develop more specific performance nutrition strategies to support her training and event preparation linked to potential sports food and supplement use.
- As an endurance athlete, she should aim to eat sufficient carbohydrate and start refuelling as soon as possible after training, when muscle capacity to refuel is at its greatest. Some of her snack food choices could reflect a greater carbohydrate content such as dried fruit to help boost her carbohydrate intake. These are easily transportable in her kit bag to be consumed on the go after her more intense training sessions.
- Her eating may need to be fitted in around the training process with smaller, more frequent meals and snacks being necessary when she is training more than once a day which is often the case with endurance athletes.
- Generally she has used her rest days well to optimise her recovery and preparation for future sessions.
- A high fluid intake should be encouraged at all times and it is noted on one of her rest days that this is low and would need to be investigated. Weight and urine-colour checks are a useful and simple way of monitoring fluid status after training. A weight reduction of 1 kg is equivalent to 1 litre of fluid loss. Frequent trips to the toilet to pass plentiful quantities of pale-coloured urine are an indicator of good hydration, whereas scant quantities of dark-coloured urine indicate poor hydration.
- These simple checks before and after exercise can be useful in determining fluid requirements post-training. As a guide, after exercise fluid losses should be replaced with more fluid than you lost (e.g. replace fluid lost with 1.5 times more than you lost) within the first 2 hours of recovery.

Strategies for pre-event
- Olivia's pre-training or competition meal should aim to top up muscle and liver glycogen stores. It should be rich in carbohydrate but low in fat and fibre and should contain a moderate amount of protein. Larger meals take longer to digest and competition nervousness can result in delayed digestion so it is important that nutritional strategies for Olivia's race are well practised and familiar.
- It is important to advise her not to experiment with new foods in competition but to use training to experiment with developing nutritional strategies to be implemented on race day.
- It is noted that her race start time is 11.00 am. She should be encouraged to eat a high carbohydrate diet the day before and ensure an adequate fluid intake, using urine colour as a simple indicator of adequate hydration status. Olivia's usual breakfast of a small glass of orange juice, porridge made with semi-skimmed milk and fruit is a good option. She may want to add a little extra carbohydrate by including a slice of toast with jam or marmalade and ensure she consumes additional fluids.
- To keep energy levels topped up and hydration adequate as she arrives at the race venue and warms up for the event, she may want to sip on a tried and tested sports drink.

Strategies for event
- As long as Olivia has prepared well for the event, there will be no need to consume any additional fluid and foods during her cross-country event due to its short time to complete.

Strategies for post-event
- It is important for Olivia to refuel as soon as possible after her race. The longer she delays refuelling, the longer it will take her to fully refuel.
- To refuel efficiently, a high carbohydrate intake is required. She should aim to consume a high-carbohydrate (at least 50 g) low-fat snack such as a bagel and jam, dried fruit or milkshake, as soon as possible after competition, preferably within the first half hour when muscle capacity to refuel is greatest.
- Olivia should then aim to eat her next meal, which should be rich in carbohydrate, within 2 hours. If her race is a long way from home, she may want to continue to consume carbohydrate-rich snack foods, or pack a wrap or pasta-based meal to consume on the journey home.
- It would have been helpful to know when she consumed the particular snacks each day around her training. She might want to incorporate bananas into her post-training recovery strategy more often as these are rich in carbohydrate and easy to eat.
- She should start rehydrating immediately. Sports drinks, either homemade or commercial, containing carbohydrate will also assist with energy and glycogen replacement. These may be particularly useful if the race has resulted in a suppression of appetite and a reluctance to eat solid foods.

Modifying use of sports food and nutritional supplements
- Some endurance athletes find sports foods such as drinks, bars and gels useful to help them meet their nutritional goals during particularly demanding periods of training and competition. For example, sports drinks are a convenient way to meet the high energy demands of training or competition.
- As Olivia does not currently consume any sports foods or supplements in her nutritional programme, she might want to consider the risks versus benefits of any sports foods or supplements that could be incorporated in to nutritional strategies pre-, during and post-training or cross-country racing such as energy drinks or gels, caffeine and beetroot juice. These all have potential to enhance endurance performance.
- It is important to remember that supplements should be safe, effective and legal. Supplements will not compensate for consistently poor food choices, but may provide a short-term solution for a nutrient deficiency, such as when travelling, until a dietary solution can be implemented.
- Olivia might want to consider the use of beetroot juice, a relatively new nutritional supplement in sport. Beetroot is rich in nitrate. After consumption, nitrate is converted to nitrite and stored and circulated in the blood. In relation to exercise performance, nitrate supplementation reduces the oxygen cost of submaximal exercise and can enhance exercise tolerance and performance and appears to represent a promising new approach for enhancing physiological responses to exercise, such as muscle efficiency and oxygenation.
- Olivia may want to consider experimenting with caffeine to enhance performance on race day. Caffeine enhances alertness and increases the time that an individual can sustain their optimal output or pace while undertaking activities. Athletes

do not need to consume large doses of caffeine to achieve performance benefits. If she wants to use caffeine to enhance performance, she should develop supplementation strategies that use the lowest effective dose. Although caffeine may enhance performance in most people, some are non-responders and some may exhibit a negative response, so this needs to be trialled in training before race-day implementation.
- If Olivia is going to consider implementing caffeine or beetroot juice on race day, she needs to trial these first in training to ensure she does not experience any undesirable side effect, particularly gastrointestinal discomfort.

Revision question 3 (pages 116–117)

Individual responses, which may include the following.

Endurance events and nutritional challenges

Endurance events challenge energy and fluid stores, so athletes should:
- aim to maximise glycogen stores by increasing carbohydrate intake during the two or three days before competition
- start exercise fully hydrated
- consider if supplements (energy drinks, bars or gels) may be useful.

Pre-event phase of training
- Many of the principles of preparing for an event mirror those of the training diet. Nutrition demands focus on maintaining energy and fluid requirements, and competing at an optimum weight, free from injury and illness.
- A pre-competition meal should aim to top up muscle and liver glycogen stores. It should be rich in carbohydrate but low in fat and fibre and should contain a moderate amount of protein as nervousness on competition day can result in delayed digestion.

Recommended meal plan leading up to the race
- For a meal plan leading up an 11am cross-country championship, I would recommend Olivia to plan her nutrition intake for the night before.
- If she takes a meal high in carbohydrates and moderate in fat and protein, these will slow digestion of the meal and allow her glycogen stores to fill up throughout the night, for example spaghetti bolognaise with peas or even a pizza with a low fat topping such as ham and pineapple.
- If Olivia eats her meal early, she should have a small bedtime snack that has twice as much carbohydrate as protein, such as a bowl of cereal with milk or a bagel topped with cottage cheese.
- On race-day, Olivia should have at least 3 to 4 hours before her race and I would recommend a reasonable-sized breakfast high in carbohydrate, moderate in protein, low in fat.
- Looking at Olivia's typical nutritional programme, familiar examples of race-day breakfasts would include cereal or porridge made with semi-skimmed milk, with a slice of toast with jam, a banana and a small glass of fruit juice.
- Olivia's pre-event meal should be made up of familiar foods and provide adequate fluids. Solid foods can usually be consumed with comfort up to 2 hours before an event, but liquid meals or carbohydrate drinks can be consumed up to 30–60 minutes before. She would be encouraged to taper training in the week leading up to the event, include a rest day, and consume more carbohydrate and fluid than normal to ensure she is optimally hydrated and fuelled ahead of her race.
- If Olivia suffers from race-day nerves and struggles to eat solid food, she should nibble on snacks that are tolerable such as cereal bars and dried fruit or try liquid meals such as smoothies.
- Sipping on sports drinks leading up to the start will help to achieve adequate hydration and tip up energy stores.

Expected outcomes from recommended nutritional strategies
- Developing sound nutritional strategies should help Olivia to train consistently and effectively to achieve the desired adaptations from her training programme that will ultimately impact on race-day performance.
- Meeting her energy and fluid requirements should help her maintain health and reduce the likelihood of illness and injury and optimise race-day performance. Developing strategies she is familiar with should give her confidence on race day that she is well prepared.